ONE
DARK
NIGHT

Rochelle Dreeben

Laurel Press
Laguna Beach, California

Photographs courtesy of the author
Cover art by Eva Darai
Book and cover design by Rosemary Boyd

LAUREL PRESS ISBN: 0-9670376-3-8

Library of Congress Card Number 2009911489

Printed in the United States of America.

Acknowledgments

I wish I could wrap this book in some teal blue tissue, present it to my mother along with a big hug, and say, "I wrote this for you, because I'm so lucky to have had you for my Mom." Since that is no longer possible, I can only hope that somewhere, somehow, in this universe, it pleases her.

I am so grateful to Mary Jane Roberts, my wise writing teacher, for just the right balance of encouragement, support, and criticism to keep me trying, and for periodically reminding me "you have a commission from your mother." Thank you, Mary Jane. Also, thank you for putting me in touch with a special group of my fellow classmates who became my informal editorial staff. They were wonderful company as well as great critics. Their comments, reactions, and good advice helped to keep me in line. They included Sue Cameron, Ruth Tresor, Erna Ferris, Burt Baum, Adele Kopecky, Judith Altschule Lieber, and Marguerite Vidales.

I'm very grateful, too, to my artist friend, Eva Darai, who created the cover illustration and suggested the title, *One Dark Night*.

I also thank Rosemary Boyd and Laurel Porter, my editors at Laurel Press, who guided me in putting all the little bits together into a readable and publishable form. Most of all, thank you to my husband and three daughters for their continued interest, support, and patience. I love you all.

Foreword

Little did I know when I took on the task of editing
Rochelle (Rachel) Dreeben's book, *One Dark Night*, how
powerfully it would affect me. Simone de Beauvoir said
that even though we might know about the holocaust
intellectually, hearing the personal details from a survivor
forces us to "live it in our minds, hearts and flesh. It
becomes our experience." (In her preface to the published
text of Claude Lanzmann's movie *Shoah*, Pantheon Books,
1985.)

While I was immersed in this project, I never knew
when something in my own life would wrench me suddenly back into Rachel's story. During that time, all my
friends heard my feeble retelling of parts of her terrifying
life during those dread years between 1940 and 1947. I
couldn't get over the fact that Rachel and I were of an
age, and while I was blithely playing with dolls and
having tea parties with my friends, sleeping safe and
sound at night in the snug home I was lucky enough to
live in with both my parents, Rachel was living in the
fiendish netherworld created by the Nazis in Poland,
losing almost everything.

Almost. Except her mother, Leonia, who was there
to protect her. I mused over what it was that allowed
Leonia and Rachel to survive when so many others
didn't. Maybe it was largely luck. But certainly also it was
courage, brains, and unflagging love. That and the brav-
ery and self-sacrifice of many others, including Rachel's

own father, who willingly relinquished his beloved wife and daughter in order to save them, snatching the chance to send them out of the Warsaw Ghetto while he stayed to fight. Rachel, in these stories, acknowledges the many who helped along the way: from their "fairy godmother," who appeared in the ghetto and picked out Leonia and Rachel to help escape when she couldn't find her own family, to Sister Bernarda, who found Polish cover for them so they could survive, to the anonymous and shadowy figures who at various times guided them to safety, relative and temporary though it might have been.

Meeting Rachel in person and seeing her in her home in Southern California somewhat allayed my dismay at her painful childhood. I marvel that she managed to outlive those nightmares she refers to in her story —a tribute to the healing power of time, perhaps, and surely that of love. Throughout these stories, one is struck by the power of love and trust, especially between mother and daughter.

Thank you, Rachel, for letting me participate in your witness to the courage, strength, humor, and devotion you and your mother manifested in your journey to safety.

Rosemary Boyd, Editor

1

Fateful Moment
Rachel, April 1943

I can feel my Dad behind me as we are climbing up the huge ladder. His warmth envelops me like a protective shield against the dark and the wind. Quietly and carefully we are climbing each step, almost like one body. His breath is reassuring on the back of my neck. The light pressure of his hands on my shoulders encourages me to keep going even though I cannot see the top of the ladder. He says I can do it. I trust him. His support thwarts my fear so that I'm not too scared even though it's so dark that I can barely see the next rung. My six-year-old legs go up another widely spaced step. He is whispering in my ear now: "Seven, eight, we are almost there, just keep going!" And still I cannot see over the wall in front of us. But he's there, still there. I can feel the coarse wool of his jacket brushing against my own coat. It has a special smell, a mixture of the cold air and the warm scent of his body that I know so well. His arms encircle me and now he is hugging me so tightly I can feel his heart beating. Now his hands caress my face, cold rough hands that always comfort me. I feel safe, so safe. I want to forget the constant sense of foreboding that keeps on bothering me. I want to keep this moment forever. But after an all-too-brief instant he picks me up high, high over the wall and the barbed wire on top of it. Then his hands slip away.

Unfamiliar arms catch me and set me down on the ground. Strange, disturbing, scary arms attached to a tall, thin shape covered in dark garments topped off by a high collar and a black knit hat. I cannot see the face but I hear him whisper, "Shh, don't be afraid." The voice is strange and not reassuring. It's definitely not my father. One of his hands takes one of mine and leads me a short distance. I do not resist. He parks me close to the trunk of an old tree, and places my own finger over my own mouth to remind me again to be quiet and motionless. Then even he disappears. But not before reminding me to stand there and not utter a sound.

Before we left our last place, both my father and my mom told me that I would have to be very silent and wait after we got over the wall. I promised I would. But it's so dark, so shadowy, so eerie. And it's already been so long. There is nothing here except the wind. It is whistling like a wolf, louder and louder and getting closer and closer. I close my eyes to block out the scariness. I put my arms around the trunk of the tree. They don't reach very far. The tree is cold and hard and uncaring. It doesn't help. I don't want to know or hear or admit even to myself how alone I feel. What happened to my dad? Why isn't he here? Why wasn't he there to catch me like I expected? Did I misunderstand what he said? Where is my mom? She went over the wall first but I do not see her. So much time has gone by, or so it seems. I strain my ears for the sound of someone coming to help me. No sound except for the wind. Maybe they forgot me. It's getting so terribly cold.

I think I hear soft footsteps. At last. They are coming closer. I hope it's for me. I hope it's someone good. A big man is next to me now and he is whispering to me to give him my hand and to go with him quietly. I don't know who he is, but it's not the same man who took me to this tree. He is speaking Polish so I don't think it's a German. I know it's the Germans that I must fear. He tells me that my mom is already waiting for me in his carriage. It's just a few steps away. I don't know if I should trust him. But there is no one else to help me. He takes my hand and we walk.

YES! My mom is there. She draws me close to her and puts her arms around me. The skin of her face is ice cold just like mine, but it feels so good against mine. I'm not deserted. My faith in her overcomes all my fright. Now I can breathe again. My blood is warming again. I don't want to think about tomorrow or even the next moment. Right now, at last, she is with me again. Just like she has always been. Always!

2

Nazi Laws
Leonia, 1939-1942

War again. Germans again. Bombs, invasion, defeat. Blown-up buildings, constant fatalities. Poland occupied again. The Germans declare they will be just and fair, that no one need be concerned except political agitators, moneylenders, and Jewish exploiters.

We are definitely concerned. We are already distressed. Our hardware store was blown up during the early bombings. Joshua went there hoping to salvage whatever he could, but looters got there before him. All he brought back were some hinges, some pairs of bent pliers, some hammers with scorched handles, and a sewerage cover blown into the rubble by the blast. Not much for all his years of work. We are lucky to have our flat at Ceglana 10. It remains intact because our home is in the part of the building behind the courtyard; the front part facing the street was destroyed.

New laws come like bullets, frequently and emphatically, telling us what is forbidden!

- *Jews must observe curfew from five o'clock PM.*
- *Jews may not eat in restaurants or go to theaters.*
- *Jews may not use public toilets.*
- *Jews may not marry Aryans.*

- *Jews may not hire Aryans.*
- *Jews over six years old must wear a yellow armband with a blue Star of David and the word "Jude" in the center.*
- *Jews must declare all personal property and possessions.*
- *Jews cannot withdraw more than 200 zlotys from banks per week.*

Our store is already gone. Nothing to declare. I went to our bank, the Peca O, and withdrew our allotted sum. My light skin and perfect Polish got me by with no problem. But when Joshua went the next week, his olive skin and Jewish accent made him a ready target for Polish hoodlums. The Germans encourage them. They took his money and beat him up so badly he was barely able to get home.

- *Jews may not own securities or gold.*
- *Jews may not own radios or telephones.*
- *Jews may not enter the central post office.*
- *Jews may not enter movie theaters.*

The same month that the Germans invade from the west, the Soviets take over Eastern Poland. Two of my brothers are there, on the Russian border, doing sales for my father. We don't know which is the worse devil—the SS or the Soviets. Between the invading armies and the barrage of prohibitions, communications are chaotic. My brothers decide that they will be better off if they can get back to Warsaw. The family is here. Their sweethearts are here too. They manage to return. My youngest brother Adam reappears as well. He had been serving with the Polish Army during the German invasion. After the Polish defeat his unit fell into total confusion. Like many others, Adam was terrified. He deserted and came home.

- *Jews must stand in a separate line to receive food rations; 2600 calories for Germans, 667 for Poles, 184 for Jews.*
- *Jews may not do kosher ritual slaughter.*
- *Jews may not participate in congregational worship.*
- *Jews may not receive letters or packages from abroad.*
- *Jews may not deal in textiles or processed leathers.*

Business is impossible. We know this means the end of my father's leather goods shop. They will confiscate it just as they did during the First World War. Whatever we can, we hide; small items like wallets or fine alligator skins can be tucked in places like false hems of garments or under the linings of coats, and hopefully sold later. There is still plenty left for the Germans when they haul away our skins, machines, metal, even the furniture. We decide to try to leave Warsaw and go to Bialystok, near the Russian border, but cannot find a way to get there. It's too late.

- *Jews may not use trains to travel between cities.*
- *Jews may not own print shops.*
- *Jews may not own furs. Furs must be handed over to the Germans.*

Winter is just beginning and already it is unusually cold. Our houses have insufficient heat. Warmth is a luxury. Outside the snowflakes camouflage the faces of the people, as they stand waiting and shivering in the wintry gusts to obey the Nazi command that they hand over their warmest possessions. There are only a few days to comply. The punishment for failure to do so is death. We hate to give up our furs even though we know we cannot wear them. Joshua takes his fur-lined jacket, my coat, and Rachel's white rabbit and buries them in the basement of our apartment house. Floors there are not cemented. "Better they should rot here," he says.

- *Jewish teachers may not teach in Polish schools.*
- *Jewish doctors may not treat Polish people.*
- *Jews may not employ Polish people in their homes*

We feel as though a lightning bolt from a dark cloud is sapping the oxygen out of our blood, and the fuel out of our bodies. So many decrees, one after another—each one squeezing the life out of us. The Poles are suffering too, but not like us, and not with us. The Jewish Agency is helpless to protect us. The Germans had set it up only to help them keep us in order. There is no one to appeal to.

- *Jews may not enter specified streets in the center of Warsaw.*
- *Jews may not own cars.*
- *Jews may not own bakeries.*

No bakeries means no bread. Life cannot go on without bread! During the First World War we could leave the city and try to go to the country where there was more food. Now we can't travel. Our shops are closed. The making of our most important staple, bread, is denied to us. Then the Germans decide that Jews need less food than a Pole, and much less than themselves. By hook or by crook bread must be brought in from outside the ghetto.

- *Jews may not use public parks or sit on public benches.*

• *Jews must step off the sidewalk upon seeing a German.*
• *Jews must close all their educational institutions.*

Through the centuries we have always held education of our youth uppermost in importance. We, "the people of the book," are commanded to close our schools. No, that cannot be—education will have to be conducted in secret.

• *All Jews from anywhere in the city must resettle to the ghetto.*
• *All Jewish money in banks will be forfeited to the Nazis.*
• *All Jewish property outside the ghetto will be confiscated.*

We are trapped here, just like in the fifteenth century, when Jews escaping the Inquisition in Spain fled to Rome only to be forced into walled ghettos there. I remember how aghast I was as a child when we studied about those times. "Is it possible that people were so horrid?" I asked my father. "Well that's in our history, that's how it was then," he replied. "But if you chose to convert, you could have your life spared, at least in theory."

But that was long ago. Now we are almost in the middle of the twentieth century. Surely the world has become more civilized now. Things can't get worse. We even rationalize that possibly it would be to our advantage to be insulated from the anti-Semitism of the Poles and the vicious rule of the Germans. Perhaps we will be given a chance to govern ourselves and simply pay extra taxes. That had been the way under Polish rule for generations. But even that isn't possible with all these rules.

Frenzy ensues. All the Poles are forced out of the area that is to be the Jewish ghetto. Almost five hundred thousand of us Jews must be squeezed in there. We may use only the trolleys that are marked with a Star of David, and then we have to pay extra. Poor people carry what they can, some in wheelbarrows, some on horses—many on their own backs. They beg and barter for any available shelter.

Our ghetto buzzes like a beehive with small factories set up by the Germans to make bullets for their war needs, with small clandestine shops, selling, bartering— anything to keep the flesh going. Germans, Poles, and some Jews take advantage of the situation. There are little workshops to make clothes and furniture and pots and pans. Almost everything is for export out of our ghetto. Getting material from outside is illegal if you are Jewish so most of the operations are shady at best. Smuggling and bribery and stealing keep the ghetto going.

Joshua tells me how loads of used clothes are brought in after dark, when secret operations can begin.

"What about the guards?" I ask, knowing every gate is guarded by Polish, Ukrainian, and sometimes German guards.

He laughs. "Yeah! Well thank God for greed. We couldn't exist without it. The guards have to be paid off, of course. The Polish ones and the Ukrainian ones are happy to have their paws smeared. The Germans are no better. Let me tell you about their 'incorruptible German honor.' I watched yesterday as a Jew was standing in the doorway haggling with a German in uniform. All was quiet and they seemed to be agreeing on some deal until a Nazi officer approached the pair. Suddenly the soldier's demeanor became arrogant and angry. 'This Jew is trying to bribe me!' he exclaimed to the officer. He pulled out his gun and shot the poor man."

I work for a while in one of the clothing factories. We are all squeezed together and work for slave wages. At the first opportunity I sneak one of the jackets we make out of the place. It is put together from many pieces of fabric, parts of old pants, bed quilts, anything that is of similar weight. All these rags are dyed the same color so that everything looks good. The inside of this jacket is stuffed with more rags, and sometimes even cardboard for warmth. It is rather bulky, but that is exactly what we want.

Joshua and I open up some seams, near the bottom and in the shoulder pads, and we enclose little cloth bags filled with our jewelry and money. It is one of the first things we grab whenever we have to leave.

Our home is located on Ceglana 10, just at the edge of the Small Ghetto, which is not quite as congested as the other part, known as the Large Ghetto. A footbridge connects our Small Ghetto to the Large Ghetto over a street that is only for Aryans. We try to avoid the bridge because German guards are almost always there looking for any reason to harass us. Still for a short while we have our own home. Though we are sharing it with my husband's sister and brother-in-law, and frequently several of my relatives as well, we are lucky. When we can sleep at all, we share our bed with two or more others. We take turns in our one bathroom to wash with insufficient water, which we save in a basin to be used to wash many hands. We cling to the hope that the German people will rebel and reestablish their humanity. We tell each other they will be defeated soon. We live on hope.

Our biggest problem is getting food. That is possible only if you can pay exorbitant prices. Many little children have paid for that food with their blood. Their blood

WARSAW GHETTO MAP

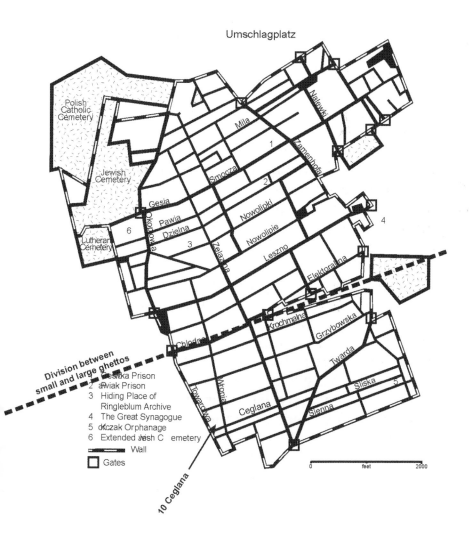

Umschlagplatz

Polish Catholic Cemetery

Jewish Cemetery

Lutheran Cemetery

Gesia
Okopowa
Pawia
Dzielna
Zelazna

6

3

Nalewki
Mila
Smocza
Zamenhofa

1

2

Nowolipki
Nowolipie
Leszno

4

Elektoralna

Chlodna
Krochmalna
Grzybowska
Twarda

Division between small and large ghettos

Towarowa
Wronia
Ceglana
Sienna
Sliska

5

1 Gesiaka Prison
2 Pawiak Prison
3 Hiding Place of
  Ringleblum Archive
4 The Great Synagogue
5 Korczak Orphanage
6 Extended Jewish Cemetery

━━━ Wall
☐ Gates

10 Ceglana

0   feet   2000

11

sustains us. Without them we cannot exist. They come through tunnels they dig under the wall. They find ways to bring in food over the rooftops of buildings that are close to the other side of the wall. They come through holes made among the bricks of the wall. Each day more and more of them are killed.

- *Jews may not attend synagogues or any place of worship.*
- *Jews may not have access to trolleys passing through the ghetto.*
- *Jews must vacate the area of the Small Ghetto, as directed by the Germans.*

One by one the Germans close this street and that street and tax us for the cost to tear down one wall and to rebuild another one that will close us in even more. The entire size of the ghetto is reduced to less than half its original size. Our own men, who are slave laborers for the Germans, are forced to do the construction. We scramble to find some other place, and then another place, again and again. With each move the congestion is worse. Every dislocation means less space, fewer items, and more difficult adjustments. Several times a week we are forced to close our windows and cover them completely with black blinds. Our light is cut off, our breeze too. There are too many people and too little air. It is hard to breathe on warm nights. We are losing contact with the rest of our families. Where are my brothers?

We become vagabonds. A couple of months here, a week there. Finally we share a room on Kupiecka Street with three other families.

The Jewish Agency must deliver thousands of Jews every day for "relocation"—five thousand yesterday, six thousand today, nine thousand tomorrow. Even those with permits are not safe if the German quota is not filled. The only ones that seem to be safe are the Jews working for German shops.

Streets are blockaded; people are seized from homes, shops, hiding places. Whole blocks are surrounded. The quota must be supplied. Terror is everywhere. Joshua and I are working for a German factory but we do not feel safe. We are afraid each time the SS comes without notice to announce more regulations, to inspect our work, to check our papers. We are terrified. We do not trust their promises. We hear they have "liquidated" Jews in other places unexpectedly. All those caught within are gone. The Germans just lie and kill.

We leave. I begin working in the soup kitchen of the apartment house on Kupiecka Street and Joshua is conscripted for slave labor outside of the Ghetto. We continue to try to stay alive.

3

Early in the Ghetto
Rachel, 1940–1941

The screen that divides our room has a lot of lacy shapes. Some look like trees in winter covered with snow. Others look like white flowers in summer gardens. I am four years old and spend a lot of time looking at them while I sit on my mattress on this side of the screen and pretend that they are real. Within the grayness of this room they are the only pretty things. I like the holes in between the threads. Sometimes when the sun is shining in the morning, the light peeks right through those openings and paints dabs of flecked color all over my mattress and the wall behind it. Some moments they all look like they are dancing. I want to dance too. I want to go out to our park and play and yell and laugh like I used to do but now we can't. We don't have a park anymore. Mom says it's too dangerous to go out. Everything is too dangerous.

Actually it is not really a screen. I think it's our tablecloth. It divides this room into our sleeping area and the rest of the space where there is an old table and some chairs. That is where we eat and do everything else. But there is nothing to do here and I have no friends. Mom let me bring only two of my dolls and two of my books because she said it was more important to have warm clothes and blankets. I don't like this place and I know

Mom doesn't like it either. She says we just don't have a choice.

I miss our home the way it was when we used to have nice rooms and plenty of space for all of us, and even my dolls too. That was at our old address, Ceglana 10, before we had to move to this ugly place. That is where this tablecloth, which is now a screen, used to cover our big table. A chandelier with shiny crystal balls hung above it. In the morning the sunshine would reflect all around that room. Sometimes my Dad would pick me up and dance all around that table with me in his arms. I loved how that chandelier sparkled, especially on Shabbat when the candles were lit. Lots of times my grandma and grandpa came over and some of my cousins too. It was a lot of fun. We all wanted to play with my grandpa. He always had good stories to tell us and to make us all laugh.

My room was bright and all my dolls and animals were very happy. My bed was soft and covered with a fuzzy bedspread. Now there's only this ugly mattress lying right on the floor with just one huge comforter for all of us. In my old house I made a pretty table for my dolls with the little china cups and saucers that my cousin Gutka gave me. I even had pretty little toy candlesticks to make it special. I dressed my dolls in fancy clothes and sometimes I took them to the park near our house. All except the special lady doll that used to be my mother's toy when she was little. Mom's uncle brought it for her from France. She was too precious to play with, so she just watched. Sometimes I pretended it was a Shabbat dinner, like when we went to our grandfather Chaim David's house. My cousins were there too. There were candles and we sang songs and there were lots of good things to eat like chicken soup and challah and apples and honey.

We could even have as much as we wanted. Now that we live in the ghetto we spend most of our time in this room with the curtain. We have to wear a lot of clothes because it's always cold here. I wish I still had my white rabbit coat that was so warm and cozy. Mom used to have a fur coat too. Mom says we couldn't bring them because we are not allowed to have furs here.

The books that I was allowed to bring have pictures of children riding bicycles and playing on swings and tumbling in the grass with their friends. Some of the pages are torn from too many readings. I know them all by heart anyway. There is no grass here. We had to leave most of my toys and games and my tricycle behind too. There is very little light here because the windows have dark shades. It is hard to read but I am learning some letters and I can write my name. I think I'm ready for school. But I'll have to wait. My mom says there are no schools allowed in the ghetto.

My grandfather and grandmother had to move too. They are living with my uncle and aunt and my cousins Mory and Gutka. Mom and I want to see them more often, but Mom says getting there is dangerous and complicated. It's always the Germans. They don't allow anything.

When we do see our family, the grown-ups are gloomy. Even Mory and Gutka are not like they used to be. Mory acts like the grown-ups, all dull and serious. Grandfather doesn't pick me up and swing me around like he used to. He doesn't tell us funny stories anymore either. Grandmother says it's because he isn't as strong as he used to be. She has changed too. She used to be plump and laughing all the time. And she had a nice dimple in her cheek especially when she was laughing. It was there even when she was yelling at us. We knew she didn't mean it. Sometimes she would holler at Grandpa too, because he was playing with us instead of making us all come to dinner.

"Chaim David!" she would holler, "You are just like Peter Pan. What shall I do with you? Don't you see what time it is? Aren't you ever going to grow up? You are worse than the little ones. When you die, we shall have to bury you among children. Then you can play with them forever." She always said that so we all laughed. Grandpa laughed too, and everybody would look at each other in that special way, and then he would make us go to wash our hands.

But now she is thin. Her clothes just hang on her and her face looks very thin. All the grown-ups are always nervous about the whereabouts of some of the rest of our family. No one has seen Uncle Adam in a long time. They talk a lot about "quotas," whatever that is. The Germans are demanding that the Jews give them a lot of our people for deportation to some other place. But no one has come back from that place to tell us about it. And they are worried about where to get food too. There is very little on the table, just some bread and sometimes soup. We never leave anything on our plates anymore. I get scared when they talk about the Germans. I don't really understand a lot. I try not to hear, but I can't help listening to their conversations.

They talk about the stores that are mostly closed and the street vendors that barely have anything to sell. And no one can afford the prices anyway. They say nobody can survive on the amount of food allowed us by the Nazis. There is no fruit. There is not enough bread. Even the cabbages and potatoes are mostly rotten and there are not enough of them either. They say that we must have smuggling because that is the only way that we can survive. It has something to do with the boys who are trying to bring in some bread from outside the ghetto.

Gutka's mom tells about a poor kid who got caught yesterday, just ten years old. The Nazis shot him like a criminal for trying to crawl past the guards with a piece of bread. Everyone was afraid to approach him. He died in the street without even a friendly hand to hold.

Grandpa's eyes dart toward Gutka and me. He gestures to change the subject. The adults stop talking but the quiet is depressing too. Grandpa gives me a limp smile and pats his knee. I know it is an invitation even before he says, "come here, Rala, and warm my knees." He knows I love being called by my nickname.

I get to sit on Grandpa's lap more than Gutka because I'm the youngest. I try to interest Grandpa in some finger games or string games. But he seems to want to just sit there and hold me tight. Mory pleads for a story. Gutka wants one too. Grandpa tells us about the other war that happened when he was young. It was called World War I. The Germans were mean then too. They took away all the goods and the tools from his leather shop. People had a hard time getting enough to eat then too. But after the war they started all over again and they rebuilt even better than before. He always makes us feel good with hope.

"See, Kinderloch," he says, "we will endure and carry on and live to tell the tale somehow again. Just like we did after the First World War. Sure it's hard now; it's always hard for us Jews. That is how we stay strong. We study and share and support each other whenever we can. Right, Mory?"

Mory smiles. He is nearly thirteen years old, almost a grown-up. He and my grandfather read big books together and study for Mory's bar mitzvah. It will be a big celebration for all of us. It will be soon. Mom says it has to be a secret because Jewish Studies are not allowed now. I hate the Germans. Everybody hates the Germans. When are they going to go away and stop making everyone unhappy?

*****

I'm excited. Finally we are going to Mory's bar mitzvah. I have never been to one before. It's very cold today so we are dressed in our warmest clothes. We walk very carefully because there are a lot of people everywhere in the streets. Some of them are sitting on the steps of the houses. They look very sad. Some are begging for food. I wish we had some to give them. Some of the people are lying on the streets. They are completely covered over, even their heads. They are not moving. They must be very cold.

It is always cold in Mory's house, just like in ours. Gutka greets us with her finger on her lips. This is to remind us that we must not make a lot of noise because parties are not allowed for Jews. Only two of my uncles and aunts are here. There are some strangers here too. Grandfather is telling us all to sit down wherever we can because there are very few chairs. Gutka and I and some of the adults sit on the mattress on the side of the room. Grandfather places a big tube on the edge of the table and he and Mory lean over it. Mom says it is the Torah.

That is where the laws for the Jewish people are written.
They are reading something I do not understand. This
doesn't look like the big celebration I expected.

Gutka and I can't wait until Mory finishes because
then we will get the cookies. There are only a few on the
table. I hope I get more than two. I don't think Mory
cares about the cookies. He is so proud of himself because
he reads beautifully. Grandfather says he has done an
outstanding job. We all watch with awe as Grandfather
takes out his prized gold chain watch. It twinkles under
the single overhead light bulb like a wand from a fairy
tale. Then grandfather says, "This is my gift to you in
honor of your bar mitzvah." Mory holds it and admires
its splendor. It radiates its shine as he turns it every which
way. He even shows Gutka and me how it opens up
when you press the button on the side, and how it has
other buttons to change the time. There are many handsome letters on the face of the watch. Mom says they are
called Roman numerals. Grandfather says he hopes Mory
remembers this day with satisfaction for the rest of his
life. Mory assures him that yes, he will always remember
this day and he will always cherish his beautiful gold
watch. I would. Then we each get a cookie. Only one. We
have to hurry back before the curfew. As we are leaving
we hear Grandfather tell Mory to be sure not to display
that watch anywhere except at home, because the Germans do not allow Jews to have gold.

The next time we go there, Gutka and I are not
allowed to go into the other room where Grandfather is
resting. Mom says it is because he is very sick. He has
typhus. Mom keeps wiping her face. Her nose is red and
her eyes are bleary. Grandma's face looks swollen even
though she is so skinny now. Mory tries to be manly but I

Leonia's eldest brother, Heniek, with his wife, Hela, and their children, Mory and Gutka. Warsaw, approx. 1940

can tell he has been crying too. So has Gutka. Everybody is so gray and sad.

The last time I see my grandmother or my cousins is at my grandfather's burial. Not many people are there. I watch as each adult throws some dirt over my grandfather's coffin. After the ceremony Grandmother looks at the stones on either side of Grandfather's grave. There are tears in her eyes and a funny look on her face. "Look" she says, "he is buried between two small children, just as I always said that he would be."

I never see my grandmother or my cousins again.

4

Pro-Life Abortion

Leonia, Summer 1942

Inside my uterus, life had sought its chance. That was last year in early 1941. What joy it would have been to be able to nurture it, to share that first laugh, to watch that first step. Normally we would have been making bets; is it a brother or a sister for my four-year-old daughter, Rachel? If a boy, would he be a rabbi or a leather goods manufacturer like my father, may he rest in peace? Either way, be it a he or a she, the child would have been a welcome addition to our family. But those were terrible, abnormal times, inhospitable to life, especially Jewish life. That baby had no chance to live. Its birth would have made the survival of Rachel, my husband, and me impossible. Even then, in this recently walled-in ghetto prison where our murderers forced us to live, where they slaughtered us individually and en masse, new life had no hope at all. It had to be terminated before the Nazis terminated us all.

Dr. Fisher, who had delivered my daughter Rachel, was still practicing in a sort of makeshift clinic. He knew me well. When Joshua and I were first married, he predicted that I would never conceive. Since my periods occurred only every six weeks or so and my uterus was badly tilted, he told us not to be too hopeful for a child.

A year later, when Rachel was born, he pronounced her a miracle that was not likely to ever happen again.

My own mother, still young in her sixties, had scoffed at that. "Nuts!" she said with a confident laugh. She had borne eight children and knew something about tilted uteruses. She assured me that we come from a long line of women with that same deformity. Her practical advice was, "The only way to be certain you have no children is to make sure that no man so much as places his hat on your bed."

Mom was right. However, neither humor nor conventional advice applies here in the ghetto, then or now. Each day the three of us are together is a miracle in itself. Who thinks about hats or worries about contraception? We are too preoccupied with the everyday survival of those of us who are still breathing. We are worried about those with whom we have lost touch. I don't even know where my own mother is, or if she is still alive. I know beyond doubt that we lack the resources, strength, and food to nourish another being.

Thank God Dr. Fisher agreed to perform that abortion. Even with minimum anesthetic and no time for rest and recovery, it went well, and I was able to recover very quickly. But that was when we still had some hope that Germany would be defeated soon, and that the world would not let us all be exterminated.

Now, at the end of this summer of 1942, we know the world has abandoned us. The ghetto lacks everything except disease and death. My own mom has disappeared, along with five of my six brothers. My father is dead of the typhus, rampant in this overcrowded and filthy ghetto. Not long ago I met a cousin of mine running like a madwoman through the streets, screaming that her twins were missing. She was hysterical. She had left them briefly in order to try to get some food. When she came back they had vanished along with everyone in her apartment building. Each day, when my husband leaves for his compulsory job for the Germans, we don't know if that will be our last moment together. Our single room, which we share with another family, is dark and dank. The only window looks out on desolation and misery. When closed, it is stifling. When opened, it brings in the stench of rotting flesh and the famished cries of those in even worse circumstances than ours. Survival is impossible on the German allowance of 184 calories per Jew, and that is only for those who are working.

Yet life is amazingly persistent. I am pregnant again. The clinic, such as it was, has disappeared. So has our friend Dr. Fisher. The sick lie failing in the streets. Mothers who are starving and have nothing more to give their children prop their newborn babies and their older children against the ghetto walls while they themselves are dying.

I must have an abortion again. One of the women in our apartment house is a physician. Dr. Sylvia is lucky. She is single without any children to worry about. Though the sick are everywhere, there is no place for her to practice. I beg her to help me. She understands.

We agree that she will try. This abortion will have to be done in the basement of this apartment house. We will have to use the cleanest towels available over an old wooden table that is standing there. There are all kinds of dangers. Lack of sterilization, lack of proper instruments or anesthesia—I am scared for myself and for my Rachel. What will happen to her if I do not recover? Suppose I get an infection and die? On the other hand, what will happen to her if my pregnancy is not terminated? I think of babies that have been suffocated by their own families as they were hiding in bunkers, knowing that the baby's cries will be fatal to all there. No! This baby is better off not even starting its life here.

I know Dr. Sylvia will try to boil the instruments as best she can. I will have to control myself and not scream. Worst of all is the ever-present danger that sometime during the procedure the Nazis will pounce upon us in one of their liquidation sweeps. We all know there is no way to predict where or when these might occur. They happen without warning, night or day, according to the whims of the Gestapo, or according to some number of victims that they are assigned to deliver that day for shipment to the "relocation camps," as they call them. They force everybody in an apartment house, or even a whole block, regardless of age or condition, to walk to the *Umschlagplatz* (collection point). From there, cattle cars take our people to places from which none ever come back. In such an event, Dr. Sylvia will have no choice but to leave me in whatever state I am in at that moment. If I cannot walk, the Germans will kill me. There is nothing to lose. Nothing. I agree.

Very early the next morning, Joshua carries Rachel down into the basement and puts her down on some old coats so that she can continue to sleep. I'm grateful that he is able to stay with us during the abortion. He holds my hand tightly as Dr. Sylvia does her work. He is my anesthetic. At least while Joshua is there, I am at peace about Rachel.

After the procedure, my husband helps both Rachel and me back up to our room. She never fully awakens. For the next couple of days I try to rest. Some of the other women in my building try to help me. Each day I have less and less pain. The operation is successful. I recover well, much to my own amazement and that of my husband.

A couple of days later when I seek out Dr. Sylvia to thank her, she is no longer there.

5

Umschlagplatz
Rachel, Summer 1942

We hardly ever go anywhere anymore, so I am happy anytime Mom and I go out. I know we only do it when Mom thinks it is very important. She doesn't tell me where we are going, but she always cautions me not to step away from her, not even for an instant. She holds my hand tightly as we walk. I don't know where we are going, but Mom must have a good reason. No one goes out without a great need. Not now when people are disappearing so fast. My mom never lets me out of her sight. I'm with her all the time, every day, all day. My dad is not with us. He has to work as a slave laborer for the Germans.

It all seems so fast. One minute we are walking quietly. We stay in the shade as close to the buildings as possible so as to not be noticed. Next minute disaster descends as SS uniforms with guns and thick black batons barricade the streets. They are yelling commands. They are mean. They are hitting some people too. Local police are helping them keep us in line. They force us to walk in the center of the street along with everyone else they have captured. Looking up into some of the downcast faces, I see dread in some and panic in all the others. I can sense the doom that is all around here. It's even worse than in the rest of the ghetto where a persistent misery has overcome the streets, the buildings, all living areas. Not even the sun dares to appear. The terror is in every hollow eye, in every shrunken face. My mother holds my hand tightly, very tightly. I know she will not let go. That is my lifeline.

My mother knows what to expect. She, like all the victims herded along with us, knows our destination exactly. *Umschlagplatz*! It is the train station at the edge of the ghetto. It is where the cattle cars arrive to collect a grim and destitute group of our people as though they were just garbage. Packed tightly, like sardines in cars that are sealed and locked to prevent any escape, they are sent away. I know from the adults' stories that they never come back.

A fence surrounds the area with a couple of openings watched by guards. I know about these guards from the stories that I have heard from conversations everywhere. Polish guards, Lithuanian guards, and the most feared of all of them, the Ukrainian guards. Historically, all are known for their meanness and brutality toward our people. There are Jewish guards too, hoping their jobs will allow them and their families to continue to have the right to live. I know my mother hates them. The Germans don't trust them. They exist in a shaky balance, trusted by nobody.

The people trapped inside the fence look miserable. Most are women, children, or old men, useless remnants about to be discarded. Blows, kicks, and shouts are going on all around them, and all around us, terrifying everyone except those that are beyond fear. All of them are thin, probably hungry. They sit on the ground, hopeless and emotionally worn out. Some have small bundles of food or clothing, still nursing a glimmer of hope that they are about to be resettled, that life will be a possibility. Some appear to be praying; some, with ashen faces, stare blankly into nothing.

Our throng is steered to the entrance where German officers play God. Their clean and pressed brown uniforms stand out in marked contrast to the shabby, gray, crumpled clothing of our own people. The Germans have well-fed bodies and ruddy cheeks. They look like a different species. They think they are. Yet not all are blond. Not all have eyes that are the preferred blue of the Aryans. Those that do have eyes that are blue-gray like the steel of their bayonets—or like the steel hooks at the ends of the whips they are cracking with so much vigor.

One by one the people in front of us are checked, interrogated, and disposed of according to the directives of the SS officers. "*Mach schnell*: Hurry up! To the right! To the left!" The line moves fast. What am I scared of? What is there to think? I am not yet six years old. I have my mother's hand. I'm holding it tight.

The little boy and his mother who are in front of us are also holding hands. He is small, just three or four years old. His mom is a thin, good-looking woman who seems full of life, strong and big boned. Both she and her son have the huge brown eyes veiled by enormous lashes common to Mediterranean people. Those eyes seem even larger because their bodies are so skinny. They approach the SS man as directed. "Boy to the left; you to the right." The mother tries to engage the sympathy of the Nazi. "I can work hard, I will do everything you say, please just let me keep my son with me."

The officer barely looks at her. He repeats his command. "Boy to the left; you to the right." When the mother tries to remonstrate with him again, he takes his bayonet and stabs the boy.

My mother's hands cover my eyes. Still I know. I hear the shock. I hear the scream. I smell the murder. I feel the horror. I know it is urgent that I be very, very good. Our turn is next. I keep my eyes down. I do not want to see. I do not want to know. I dread hearing the awful command. The words fall like hammers. They are in German, which I do not understand, but I know they are bad. I know that from the meanness and the sneer in the voice. I know that from the leather-gloved hand that points its index finger at us like we're just worms. Like it might be contaminated by us. "Child to the left; you to the right!"

I sense my mother's hesitation. I think she is about to protest like the lady in front of us. Before she has the chance to utter a word, that human-shaped gloved hand takes out a whip with a metal hook at its end and strikes my mother in the face. Blood springs out of her mouth and covers her face. An ugly red line is developing near her ear. Her tongue is checking a tooth that is loosened. I am terrified. Did I do something wrong? Should I have gone to the left? My mother's hand continues to hold mine firmly.

At that moment the SS brute is called to a telephone. Another one comes to replace him. While the change of guards is taking place, a Jewish policeman tries to persuade my mother, "Let her go. Give yourself a chance to survive. Some of us must still live when this war ends. Let her go." My mother's hand still holds mine determinedly.

The new officer takes over. "You to the right; kid to the left," he barks. My mother can hardly talk, but she says, "I want to go to the left with my child." The man gives her a contemptuous look and points us both to the left. We go to find a space on the ground among the wretched women and children who were also sentenced "to the left."

We sit there, my mother's face still bleeding and swelling. She wipes it with her sleeve. She has difficulty talking but she is reassuring me with her eyes that she is okay. She is watching the guards. One of them, a Ukrainian policeman, brings a cup of water to a frail old woman not far from us. What an extraordinary act of kindness! Especially from a Ukrainian. Although they are known as the cruelest of our assailants, here is one who obviously is not glorying in his job. My mother pulls me toward her and tells me to be sure to do as she says. We walk over to that Ukrainian guard and she says to him, "My daughter is very shy. May we walk over to the edge near the fence, so she can relieve herself there? He looks at us intently, then extends his arm, and points toward an area of the fence where we are to go. "*Idziej*," he says, "*Idziej*, go!"

We walk slowly in the direction he indicated, and then my mother realizes that there is an opening in the fence. It is not guarded. Did he point us there on purpose? Was he looking the other way to give us a chance? Would he shoot?

We continue to move slowly toward it. Then suddenly I feel a new urgency in her hand. We speed up. She is pulling me at just the right pace. Suddenly I understand as I hear her whisper, "Don't look back; don't make a sound; move quickly now. Stay with me."

The unguarded opening in the fence is small and not easily visible from where the masses of our people are gathered. We sneak through it without a backward look and walk on to the street. We are free! At least for the moment we have escaped deportation. The ghetto and the Germans still surround us, but that Ukrainian guard has given us another day's reprieve.

The area is not far from Mila Street, where one of my mom's brothers is working with the Jewish resistance. I cannot remember how we got in, or who let us in. But the urgency is still there. We must be hidden just in case some SS should be looking for escaped Jews. We are helped up a ladder onto a shelf high up in a storage closet where we sit for many hours, cramped, quiet, but alive. We are saved, even if just for the moment, even if just for the day, because of the kindness and the courage of a Ukrainian guard who said *"idziej."*

6

Thank God for the Soup Pot
Rachel, Fall 1942

Rachelka, my child, my mom is saying as she feels my head, "you are too sick to come with me. You will have to stay here and keep as warm as you can. Don't leave the room no matter what happens. You know that I have to work down in the kitchen. Scream if anyone tries to make you leave this room. Scream as loud as you can, even though your throat hurts. If you scream, you can be sure I'll come to you."

Staying in bed is wonderful. It's all I want. For several days I have had to go to my mom's workplace with her while feeling awful. My head feels like someone is banging inside of it. It hurts to even open my eyes. I am hot and cold and my throat is so sore. There is no question of a doctor or any medicine. But just being allowed to stay in bed is very good. I can now go back to that half-asleep state induced by my high fever.

Still, I understand my mother's warning. German evacuation sweeps are a constant worry that has everyone anxious all the time. I have heard the women in the kitchen talk about it a lot. Everyone is always worried. We don't know where the people are taken, but we know that no one is ever heard from again. There is never an hour or a place when we can feel safe. Though I am less than six years old, I realize the danger. The very word *Umschlagplatz* is enough to remind me of a terrible evil.

My mother has no choice. The Germans allow only able-bodied workers the right to live. She has to hurry downstairs to the main floor of the apartment house where the community kitchen is located. In the center there is a metal trashcan in which the women discard the most inedible parts of the vegetables that are supplied to them. Potatoes and turnips are the most frequent fare, plus sometimes cabbages, and rarely carrots. Whatever can be salvaged is thrown into the large cauldrons that sit against the innermost wall of the room. Hunger will garnish the flavor. At the end of the day, all will share the soup. Not a drop will be left.

My mother knows that anyone coming or leaving the building has to pass by the kitchen. It is right next to the entrance foyer so anyone passing there, especially a German, is sure to be heard. Certainly the chaos usually created by the Nazi thugs cannot be ignored. But no one can forget the one time when the Nazis came and went and were not heard.

There were a number of us children living here then with the remnants of our families—maybe fifteen or more of us who were still too young to work. We hung around our mothers in the kitchen without much to do. But it was nice to be together. One day an official proposed that the kids would be better off in another room with some supervision from one or two of the mothers. Maybe even some toys and some activities could be arranged. His concern impressed some of the women. They thought it was a great idea. They welcomed the diversion for their children. But not my mom. "My child stays with me!" she insisted and never vacillated.

The so-called school was created, and all the other kids were allowed to go. All except me. My days in the kitchen consisted of just sitting there and listening to the women's chatter or occasionally being asked to pick up a potato or a piece of fallen food that could not be wasted. Sometimes I heard the other women chide my mom for her selfishness and lack of consideration for my needs. Her answer was always the same. "Rachel stays with me."

Weeks went by but nothing changed my mother's mind. She was resolute. No matter what might happen, we would be together. And though I would have welcomed the opportunity to be with other children, I trusted my mom and was comfortable in the security of being near her. I stayed in the kitchen.

How had it happened? No one knew. After about three weeks, when the women went to the school to pick up their children, the room was empty. No one was there. No one! Oh my God, the children were gone! Vanished!

There was no one to ask, and no need to ask. The devastated mothers knew it had been just another ruse by the Germans. A ruse to make the murder of their children easier.

There I was, the only child left in the building. In soundless misery the women continued their toil. There was no more of the small gossip that formerly lent some hope. Red swollen fingers labored on, ignoring cuts and blisters. The silence was oppressive even to me. Memories of children, families, and festivities, all gone forever now, traumatized the women. There was hardly any conversation, no reason for hope or courage. They knew their children were dead.

Today, because I am feeling so sick, my mother has an extra concern. Typhus is spreading fast under the awful ghetto conditions. At the very least, I have to have some rest. However, should there be a Nazi sweep, Mom doesn't want us to be separated. As she leaves me by myself, she knows that I understand her fear and her directions. The high fever makes me quite sleepy and not too alert most of the day. Never for a moment do I feel deserted. I feel cared for and grateful for permission to stay in bed, huddled under the warmth of our fat down comforter.

This down comforter that is over me is not elegant. Made for cold Polish winters, it is intended to fit a single bed, and it looks more like a huge, very full pillow. It is filled with lots and lots of down. When it is puffed up, it is almost as tall as I am. Though ragged and soiled, it has managed to survive the many moves we have had to make. It faithfully continues to perform its only mission, which is to keep us warm. For that it is our highly prized possession. No one would willingly give up this treasure. Even I know it can mean the difference between life and death.

The day dissolves for me, as I lie half asleep and luxuriously warm. Our mattress is directly on the floor just to the right of the entrance to the room. My mother and I share that mattress and our wonderful comforter. Cuddling together with her at night is the best time of the day for me. My father joins us too, when he is lucky enough to come back at night. My father and other slave laborers are forced to empty Jewish residences of all their furniture and stuff. He tells us that anything that is good or useful is sent to Germany. Besides our mattress and an old wardrobe, there is almost nothing in this room. Just me under my down.

In the middle of the afternoon, the usually silent and deserted street outside explodes into chaos with the noise of gunfire, motorcycles, barked orders, shouts, and screams. I must hide quickly. Where? The wardrobe? It doesn't even have rags to crawl under. There is only one choice. I slide deep under my down comforter and try to puff it up by kicking it. Then I make myself as small as possible and hold it with my toes and my fingers. The hardest part is to make my heart stop thundering. With all my strength I hold down the comforter and concentrate on quieting the beating of my heart.

Heavy boots thunder up the stairwell. The door flies open and smashes against the wall near my head. Good! Maybe it will hide the thumping from my chest. I hear the wardrobe door open and slam shut. There is a long moment of hesitation. Then the boots come toward me. A kick shakes the mattress. I will not make a sound. I try not to breathe. Something tugs at the down near my head. With all my strength I strive to hold it down even more securely. I must do it without moving my body. Just my fingertips and my toes must hold it. Another endless moment while I will myself to be nonexistent. My eyes are shut as tight as possible. I hold my breath. Then finally I hear the boots thunder away and out of the room. The door slams shut. Outside the door there are shouts in German.

I can breathe now. I think I am saved. Is it possible that The Boots really thought there was no one here? Is it possible that there was a humane being inside those boots, even though it was a German one? Is it possible that he chose not to know? Where is my mother? Did she escape? Will I be alone now? Better not to think. Just sleep. I can go back to sleep. There is nothing to be done. Sleep.

When I awake, it is dark. My mother is sitting next to me. Incredibly, she too has been saved. She tells me that even as the others were herded out of the kitchen room, she looked frantically for a possible hiding place. There was only one place that suggested itself to her—the soup cauldron. Thank God it was empty. In the chaos and confusion of the stampeding women, she climbed into it without being noticed. There she curled up as best she could and managed to cover herself with the lid. It was freezing in that metal bucket. She was afraid that her chattering teeth would give her away. And where was Rachel? She concentrated intently, listening for the sound of my voice. Nothing. She knew that I would scream if I were taken, but even if I didn't, she could find me at the *Umschlagplatz*.

She could not leave the cauldron until the search was definitely over. Like the hunted fox, she had to out-trick the hunters. She stayed there, freezing, for a long time, just in case someone searched the rooms once again. What if the Germans pretended to leave, but were still hunting?

Finally, just as she was getting out of the cauldron, she came face to face with one of those Jewish policemen, "capos" as they are called, who carry out the dirty work of keeping the Jews in order. Startled, they looked at each other in amazement. Before he could even say anything, she attacked, "My brothers are in the underground, and if you're thinking of turning me in, be sure they will take revenge on you and your family."

"Ma'am, I'm Jewish too. I only do this job to keep my own skin. I do not want to harm you. We're all in a terrible fix together. As long as it's just the two of us, why would I turn you in? Here, let me help you out of this pot. I wish you luck." He left the room.

My father comes back that night from his slave labor. Once I was the only child left in the building. Now the three of us are the only human beings left alive in this hollow place that was once full of families. I hear my mother and father talk about how lucky we are, but I sense the undertone of their fear. "I feel like we're the ghosts of the past," Mom says. We hug each other, the three of us under the luxurious warmth of our down comforter.

7

Joshua Szyfka
Leonia, Early 1943

The first thing that attracted me to Joshua was his dark shiny eyes. They were like the eyes on Egyptian paintings—wide, black, somewhat prominent, and intense. But what I saw there was a kindness and a twinkle of humor. Then, as his lips widened for a hearty laugh, the whiteness of his teeth stood out in contrast to his smooth olive skin. I couldn't wait to touch him. That was just seven years ago. That was that wonderful time when romance was on my mind.

I consider how lucky I am to have him now, though who knows for how much longer. Even this awful last year had some happy moments whenever he was with us. Occasionally he still had the strength and inclination to play with Rachel, and she adored every moment with him. She crawled all over him, caressed and hugged him as though she had a special intuition that only she could still take away his sadness. She would put her pudgy fingers on his mouth and command, "Make a laughing face." But if he wouldn't, she would stuff a finger in his mouth and tell him that if he was hungry he could eat it all up. He would suck on it for a minute then tell her it was the best meal he had ever had and now he was not hungry any more, so she could take it out. Then it was pure joy to hear those wonderful notes of a child's giggle. We could not resist her joy.

Sometimes they still tumble on our mattress, in temporary oblivion, forgetting just for an instant our lack of food, our meager tattered surroundings, our over-crowded room, and our perilous situation in this ghetto. But now such moments are very rare. There is no laughter anywhere. Now we listen for different sounds. Sirens, the rat-tat-tat of machine guns, Nazi evacuation commands.

Now only survival interests me. Survival consumes me and Joshua and everyone around. We cannot overlook, even for a minute, our situation. Even Rachel can no longer make Joshua forget himself. I know that only this moment is ours. We should make the best of it. I should encourage Joshua in his ability to play like a child.

Sometimes I watch Rachel as she just sits and plays with her hair. Even though it is no longer as smooth and shiny as it was when we had sufficient water and soap, she still loves to touch and play with the strands. It's her security blanket. It's her only amusement. But it reminds me of our better days, when normal conveniences and even playthings were available to her. That was when Joshua and Rachel checked out each new toy, each new food, or a silky new fabric that Rachel enjoyed touching. "Is it as silky-smooth as your silky-soft hair?" he would tease her.

Rachel always loved the touch of smooth things, or the feeling of her own sleek locks. When there was nothing else, we were glad that she had something right on her own head that was always ready to give her comfort. Smells excited her too, particularly any cosmetics and perfumes that I used to wear. When I still had those, she would apply some to herself or to her dolls. If Joshua was around he too got a dose. After she got herself all primped up she would say, "Daddy, you will be my prince and I will be your princess," or, "Daddy, I am the princess and you are my slave." He would laugh, pick her up in his arms, throw her high up near the ceiling, and they would both dance away.

He is so much like my own father. Like him, Joshua has always had the ability to abandon himself completely when he plays with a child. When he and Rachel were done tumbling, and her head was snuggled into the groove of his neck, and his dark curly hair intermingled with her light brown curls that were all over his face, and her tights and little skirt have slipped off her stomach and exposed that belly button, it was the most superlative picture of total happiness that I remember. That's how I like to recall them, deliriously blissful and totally relaxed in our old home.

How different is the present from what we had envisioned then. Our concerns then seem so trivial today. When we were first engaged, Joshua worried that our income would be very modest because he needed to support his parents. And we also had to wait a year so that his older sister would be married first. The rules of society had to be obeyed. I hated the wait, but he was worth it. We did not count on this war.

Joshua opened up a small hardware store, the first to sell stainless steel goods in our area, and he did well. We purchased a small flat on the third floor of Ceglana 10, and I became pregnant there. When I felt particularly unwell or tired, he carried me up to our own special nest and commanded me to rest while he took care of every-thing. After Rachel was about six months old, his shoulders became her favorite form of transportation. Up and down the stairs went the horse and his rider. He was always full of energy and zest. He would grab me and say, "C'mon, let's dance to this great tempo music on the radio." When awake, Rachel would force herself in for a threesome. We would all laugh and dance together with Rachel perched on his one arm and I wrapped in the other.

Even after we were forced into this ghetto, and the store he had worked so hard to establish was pulverized in the initial bombing, and he had to settle for whatever labor or sales that he could find—even when he had to do compulsory labor for the Germans—he still retained his vigor. But gradually he lost weight. His posture suffered, along with his self assurance. His usual heartiness waned. I missed his magic laugh. Not even his remarkable mirth and optimism could hold up as the Nazi grip tightened. He knew that all his prowess and loyalty were not enough to protect us from the coming disaster.

Earlier in the war he had hoped that by working for the Germans he could shield us. It was the only way to get permits that entitled one to avoid the deportations. He, like the other slave laborers, cleared rubble, worked in machine shops, made items for our enemy's war effort. One of the homes that Joshua was forced to dismantle was the home of a relative where we had enjoyed many happy hours. That night he was more shaken than usual. He told me that the silver, the piano, the picture frames were all destined for Germany. Never again would those candlesticks shine at a Shabbat dinner. That violin would never again play *Bei mir bist du schein*, or any other Jewish song. The portraits of generations of ancestors, some of them ours, would be ashes, just like the exiled inhabitants.

Occasionally Joshua encountered some humane behavior even among his German guards. On one occasion a soldier gave him two eggs and an apple, saying, "Someday the tables will be turned, and then, when it is our turn to starve, I pray that some kind man will have mercy for my family." Joshua had hoped that day would come in time to save us, but his optimism is now dead. Everyone in the ghetto feels hopeless.

The deportations during this past summer of 1942 have reduced us to only a small part of our original population. We are trapped with meaningless "permits," with ruses and with lies, with promises that are broken at the caprice of the Gestapo. Joshua's parents, a brother, and two sisters are all missing. My own mother is missing too and so are most of my six brothers. Even those people still remaining are segregated into separate areas. It is very difficult to meet or to communicate. Up until now there has been a lot of disagreement between our leaders regarding how to handle ourselves in order to survive. Shall we hope for the world to save us? Shall we persuade ourselves that if we obey the Germans we might have a chance? But dissent between the Jewish leaders is finally gone. We all know that the Germans mean to annihilate every one of us Jews. We can die fighting, or we can just die.

Only the young and the strong still remain. Ironically, the scant food smuggled in by the few remaining "workers" is more ample for our drastically diminished population. Briefly, only because of their dire need for experienced labor, the Nazis are permitting a relative slowing in their "deportation" rate. We know the time to plan and to fight will be soon and it will be short.

Our first revenge already took place on our own Jewish police, the ones who had been most brutal in carrying out the Germans' orders and in assisting the SS. We have contacted the Polish underground in the hopes of getting some aid from them. The results are most disappointing. Little love is lost between the Poles and us.

Early this year, when a new wave of deportations began, we Jews were ready. This time we were not the lambs the Germans had expected to take to slaughter. Our own men and women and boys and girls surprised their soldiers with handmade grenades, and they ran away. That was our own first triumph of resistance.

But we know they will be back. We have improvised hiding places and shelters in cellars, attics, and tunnels. We have spent nights preparing bunkers. This January when our men attacked and killed some of the surprised Germans, we took their weapons. In the heat of that brief uprising, those who were already rounded up for deportation and waiting at the *Umschlagplatz* were able to run away and disperse. That battle belongs to us, the Jews! For the first time in memory we Jews are resisting. We know we are doomed and still we are proud!

8

Our Fairy Godmother
Leonia, Early Spring 1943

This ignominious winter of 1943 is coming to its dark end. We are at an end too. We are cold. We are numb. We are shattered by the callousness and cruelty of our fellow men. The world and our God have deserted us. Unless there is a miracle, we are destined for total destruction. Miracles are in very short supply.

Rachel and I and the women huddled with us in a single room feel bleak. This house, which had been evacuated a short time ago, has been reinhabited by escapees from other places. I still have my daughter Rachel. Even my husband is still alive. Though each of us has evaded the German traps and deceptions, we know and don't even try to repress the knowledge that in the end there will be no way out. There are so few of us left. If any of my brothers or cousins are still alive, I don't know where they might be. Even Rachel, just six years old, feels the doom. Apathy pervades all our existence.

Who could have known that we have a fairy godmother? She comes from beyond the ghetto, the Aryan side, where life is also difficult, but not impossible. There, she has access to better food and clean water. There, children are still enjoying school and music and amusement rides in parks located just over the ghetto wall.

There, people still take walks along the river and see trees that bloom in the spring.

But here she is, this apparition from that beyond. Her face is young. Her eyes are old. They are startling, Irish-blue eyes, made to enrapture suitors at balls and dances. Now they are scrutinizing eyes, used to assess danger, to evade capture. Her short, straight nose is red from the cold. Wisps of blonde hair peek out of her gray scarf. She is not tall, but her carriage gives her stature. She carries herself with a self-assurance that states, "Don't mess with me, I'm not Jewish!" But we know better. She is one of our own.

"I am looking for my sister," she tells those of us huddled together in the cold room. "My sister and her baby boy, where are they? Do any of you remember a young blonde woman with a three-year-old boy?"

Vacant eyes focus on her. She goes to recheck the room where she had last seen her sister, then returns. Her jaw is set tight. Her eyes are hard but dry. Two blue veins beat erratically on the side near her eyebrows. Her parched upper lip is quivering above the space of her missing tooth. I wonder if she lost it like I did to the craze of a Nazi whip.

"My sister, her name is Sarah; she has blonde hair and blue eyes just like me. She was still here three weeks ago. Her little boy is only three years old. He was not circumcised. Have any of you seen them? Can anyone tell me what happened to them?"

Some murmurs. "Yes, they were here. They're gone."

Dead silence. No tears. No exclamation. No need for explanation. No time for sentimental indulgence. We all know their fate.

She looks around and her gaze settles on Rachel and me. For a moment she seems to be deep in thought, as though trying to make a decision. Finally she takes a deep breath, and with her eyes still fixed on us she asks, "How good is your Polish?"

"Just as good as yours, as you can hear."

"And your little girl's?"

"It's her only language."

Her eyes examine us again. They calculate the color of our skin, our hair, our noses, and our speech. Can we pass? Can we pass as Aryans?

But her mind is still struggling to accept what has happened to her sister and her nephew. She tries once again. "The last time I saw my sister Sarah and her baby, it was here. I left them here in the ghetto until I could find a way to save them. I had to arrange for false papers and a place to hide them." Her teeth are clenched. A deep breath escapes from her chest. Her eyes are watery, but just for a moment. Finally she chokes out that to which she must resign herself. "I see it is too late for them." She looks around the room and her eyes settle on Rachel and me again. "I'm going to save you and your child in their place."

I feel my blood circulating again. Goose pimples cover my arms. Is it possible? "Can you really do it? I'll give you everything I have."

"I don't want your money! If you have any jewelry, keep it. It might come in useful later. Now I have to go back again and change some things. I will try to get you false papers. I think I can do it. You have to stay here until I work it out. A week, maybe ten days." She tells us to call her Basia, a typical Polish name, though it is clear to us that she is Jewish. Will she be any more successful with us

than she was with her own sister? Does she really have
the contacts and the power to make a difference? Even
though she looks gentile and is armed with excellent
forgeries attesting to her Aryan identity, we all know she
is still risking her life. And as for us, will we still be here
and alive in a week or ten days?

There has been a lull in the Nazi deportations since
January. That was the time of our own first triumph of
resistance. But we know they will be back soon.

When Joshua comes back from today's forced labor,
I tell him the good news. He is overjoyed. Those big black
eyes that I fell in love with are excited again. He switches
from Polish to Yiddish, the language most comfortable for
him. I can see that his head is spinning, looking for ways
to make our escape more secure. But as for himself, he
will not even try. He is convinced that he has no chance
to survive, not with his Semitic looks. Not with his cir-
cumcision. He must stay and fight with the resistance.

"I do have a chance to kill a couple of the bastards.
If I can do that and know you and Rachel are safe, I'll die
content."

We make plans. I'll take the jewelry that I had sewn
into my coat a long time ago. Joshua won't let me take
any pictures of him. He insists it would be too suspicious
to have a photo of someone with his Semitic looks. From
now on he will be staying here with us as much as possible. He intends to leave only to help make weapons for
the resistance. If at any time Basia shows up and we have
to leave without saying good-bye, he tells me not to
hesitate. "Go! If possible let me know you made it."

Ten days later, even as our hopes are waning, our
blessed Basia reappears. She tells us what we must do.
"Three days from today, on Thursday, the guards at the

ghetto wall overlooking the Saski Gardens will be distracted. There will be no moon and it is dark there because of the canopy of trees. You must find a ladder and get it to the wall at exactly eleven PM. Leonia, you will go over it first. The child must be lifted over the top of the wall and over the barbed wire. She will be caught on the other side. You must make her understand that she is not to cry out or make any noise, no matter what. Both of you must stand under the darkest part of the garden, but not together. Our man will guide each of you to a different tree. Should one of you get caught, the other one must not reveal herself. Make sure the child understands all this. A man who will call himself Jan will come to take you to his place as soon as he feels he can do so safely. There is always the possibility of a trap."

In the first week of April, just three days before the first night of Passover, we are ready. Joshua and I have been coaching Rachel as to what will happen and what she must do. He has spent extra time with her. She loves sitting on his knees and soaking up his warmth and his charm. She trusts him completely. For him these moments are his final gifts. He does not explain that he will not be going with us.

On the fateful night I go up first. With Joshua's help I get over the top. I'm glad it's so dark he can't see the emptiness and the turmoil in my heart. There is no time for tears or another hug. He is already out of my sight as he climbs down the ladder to pick up Rachel. I know I must follow the man who is waiting for me to take me to my tree. I hear nothing, but I know he is now giving Rachel his last hug, like he gave me, and that his arms are around her, comforting her, but she does not know she will never see him again. I can feel his heart beating just like mine, his insides tortured, his voice hoarse as he is saying to her, "Now jump, and remember to be very, very quiet."

I watch from behind a tree as the man who guided me also catches her and guides her to a different tree. I know his arms are strange to her. His smell is unfamiliar. His hands are cold. She must be frightened. He is not her father. I know he is telling her again, "Stand here and be very still."

I want to leave my space behind my tree and comfort her, but I cannot. We have to follow directions. It is terribly dark here. Even though the two different trees we're standing by are probably less than fifty feet apart, we cannot see each other. We feel only the wind and the mist and the fear. A century seems to go by until Jan emerges from the night shadows. He knows exactly where to get me, then Rachel. He has done this before. With a finger to his lips he gestures for me to go toward his horse and wagon. Shortly afterwards he brings in Rachel. We are together again. Rachel is trembling top to bottom. Her teeth are clicking.

"Where is my Dad? Why isn't he here?"

I hug my daughter close to me. Inwardly I am choking. I am unable to answer her. I must be positive. We made it. We are safe. We have a chance to live.

Without a word Jan drives us to his apartment house. He is the manager there, and like all managers, he occupies the basement apartment. This is an important job in Warsaw. An apartment manager is responsible for making sure that no one comes or goes without proper identification, that no Jew finds refuge there, that everyone's papers are in order. In the basement where he hides us, he also has concealed equipment to forge documents. Joshua and I have heard of an organization called Zagota, organized to help save the remaining Jewish children. I wonder, *Is he part of this organization? Is Basia?*

She told us that once we reached the Aryan side, she would no longer be our contact. Jan tells us that a Sister Bernarda will be our guardian angel from now on. She will come in a day or two. There will be no time for getting acquainted. We must trust her and accept her instructions. For me, it will be a job as a housekeeper for some Aryan family that Sister will arrange. For Rachel, it will be a place in a convent school where she will live as an orphan.

Just a few days later, in mid-April of 1943, Sister Bernarda comes to take Rachel to the convent Niepokalanek. She looks every bit like a guardian angel. She is dressed in a voluminous white habit that barely allows room for eyes, nose, and mouth to show. Her presence is noble. Most of the Polish population reveres the Catholic sisters. Even most of the Germans show them some respect.

She is all business. It is the custom of Polish Catholics to name their children after saints. I am renamed Basia Siudetska, an unmarried and uneducated woman from a small town. Rachel will be taken to the sister's convent, a school for girls. I must not ever try to visit there. She cautions us over and over, "Do not ever tell anyone that you are Jewish." To Rachel, she keeps repeating, "Remember that you cannot ask about your mom, because you know that you are an orphan." We both understand that there will be no way for us to see each other. We will not even be able to write an occasional letter. There must be absolutely no communication between us. Any attempt to see each other would be too dangerous.

I bend down and put both my hands on my Rachel's shoulders. I try to smile but I can't. I say, "Listen to Sister, do what she says. She will keep you safe."

Another final moment—I wonder, *Will this be our last moment together ever? Will my daughter become one of those Catholics who hate Jews? Will she be taught that we are Christ-killers? If we both stay alive, will I, and our own people, be repulsive to her? My father's face comes to me. I hear his voice, "First of all, live!"*

Sister says they must hurry! I remind Rachel again that she must be brave and not worry about me. She must not ever even ask about me because I am supposedly dead. She understands death. She understands that both our lives depend on keeping our secrets. Both our hearts are pounding as she hugs me back. She is holding me so tight I know she is afraid to let me go. I pry myself away from her and I tell her again to be a good Catholic girl.

"How long will I have to be there?" she asks, still holding onto me. She is trying not to cry. How is it that my eyes stay dry? Soon I will not be able to hold back tears. I promise that just as soon as I can, just as soon as this war is over, I will come for her.

Sister holds her hand and speaks kindly as she leads her away. My Rachel's new name will be Teresa Kurek. Sister Bernarda immediately begins to indoctrinate Teresa into Catholicism, "You will be taught wonderful things about Jesus Christ. You must learn quickly, and never mention anything at all about your real past or ask about your mom or dad. Remember, they are dead."

9

Introduction to the Convent
Rachel, Spring 1943

The whiteness here is magical. It permeates every pristine corner. It glides on the waves of northern light coming in through these third-story dormer windows. It is pure, constant, untainted by any sunlight. It frames and lends importance and tranquility to everything in this room, especially the cross on the wall and our Mother Superior who is sitting on the single chair in the middle of the room.

Her habit has many folds of cream-colored linen. They all reflect that light bouncing within the room and give her an aura of holiness. She sits in a stately fashion, looking very grand. On her chest is a big cross, just like the one on the wall. Mother Superior and the room suit each other. I like that.

From within the oval opening of her habit, only the barest features are visible: perfect skin, a straight nose, and deep blue eyes that are framed by dark-rimmed glasses. They gaze at me with concern.

I'm a small and thin six-year-old, so insignificant in all this splendor. Sister bids me to sit on her lap, but I'm afraid to soil her garment. I'm also afraid to disobey. I place myself carefully so as to avoid creasing the spotless linen, and I try to be as light as possible. Her arms enfold me with care.

"Are you happy here, Tereska?" Her voice sounds clear, melodic. I like her use of the affectionate form of my newly acquired name.

I nod. My name is still awkward to my ears. It was given to me in honor of St. Teresa. It's part of my secret, which is part of my past. I must be careful to respond to it in a natural manner. I must forget that other name,

Convent Szymanow, located on the outskirts of Warsaw. This picture is taken after it had been rebuilt following the ravages of the war.

Rachel, or my nickname, Rala. They could provide a clue to my real identity. Even Mother Superior does not know. Or does she?

"God has chosen you to be brought here to our convent so that you may be saved. His name is Jesus. He has a special love for children like you."

Neither heaven nor Jesus has any significance for me. But I do want to be saved, especially from the Nazis.

I'm well aware that that is the reason for my being here. I listen for more. "Yes, Sister," I say as I have been taught to do.

"Those of us who love Jesus and who pray to him are the only ones who will go to heaven. Heaven is a wonderful place where good Catholics go after they die."

"All good people go there?"

"No Tereska, only those who have accepted Jesus into their lives. Only those who have believed and prayed through Jesus. You see, all the people in the world are born sinners. Only our Gentle Savior, Jesus, can save them."

"Even babies who haven't done anything?"

"Yes. Everybody. You see, everybody is born with sin. That is why Jesus, the Son of God, wants to give them a way to go to heaven. That is why he sacrificed himself. He died on a cross to pay for the sins of the world. You are lucky to have the chance to get to know him."

I'm thinking of my mother. She has never mentioned Jesus. Has she ever heard of him? I don't know if either she or my father is alive. Will either of them be saved from the Nazis? If not, can either of them go to heaven? I'm supposed to be a Catholic orphan. I cannot ask these questions.

"What about someone who never heard of Jesus. Can they get into heaven?"

"No. But they might have a chance if they were very good. Then they would go to purgatory, which is a place that allows you to wait for the time when you are fit for heaven."

"How about if you know about Jesus but you are a bad person?"

"Well, that is the wonderful thing about Jesus. As long as you believe in him and confess your sins and ask for his pardon, he will forgive you. Jesus is so kind and caring. Then you still go to heaven."

"How about people who were born before Jesus?"

"They too will have to go through purgatory."

I must be careful. I cannot ask about Jewish people. Sister says Jesus is loving and caring. But is he a fair or just God? How can it be that good people will be punished when they did not have the chance to know Jesus, and if this God is merciful as Sister says, then would he punish people for not knowing him? Is it possible that this God forgives those who know him and pray to him even if they are killers? Killers of my own people, good people?

"There is a lot for you to learn with us, Tereska. We will teach you how to pray not only for yourself but also for people everywhere. You will be baptized and christened. We will prepare you for confession and for communion. You will learn all the wonderful stories about Jesus. Soon you will love him. Now go outside and play awhile before dinner."

Outside is already heaven. Perfume of early spring fills my nostrils. How different from the smell of burning cinders that permeated the ghetto my mother and I escaped from just a few weeks ago. There, nothing existed but cement, ruins, filth, and starving people in misery. I view an expanse of greenery and trees such as did not exist in the ghetto. Their branches go right up to the fence that surrounds the convent. A regular fence, not a threatening one with barbed wire and broken glass on the top. Not at all like the one that my Mom and I climbed over to escape from the Warsaw Ghetto.

Life seems safe here. Even the sounds are soothing.
Birds are busy with songs and preparation for their nests.
Harmonious singing can be heard from inside the chapel
where the sisters are chanting in soft mellow tones. Their
voices are calm, peaceful. (Little do they, or anyone in the
convent, know that Nazi officers situated just across the
street are eyeing this property for their own headquar-
ters, or that our remaining tranquil time here will be very
short.)

There is some light laughter and giggling near me.
A few girls have gathered around an ash tree and I wonder if we are allowed to climb it. I watch as some of them
place three fingers at the top of the very young leaf
clusters and strip them all at once with one swish of their
wrists. Now they have fragile rose bud bouquets of ash
leaves. So fragile that any movement of their fingers
could make the buds disappear. Puff, just like that, the
leaves will lose their base of support. Puff, just like that,
they will scatter and die.

Sonia is making a crown for her hair. She pins two
leaves together with an evergreen needle and adds more
leaves until the crown fits. She tops it off with a yellow
dandelion. Soon everybody is copying her. I hope that
someday I will be like Sonia.

Some of the older girls who can read are studying
little white books. They are called "catechism." They must
be very important. I will learn to read and study the
catechism and concentrate on fitting in here. This is a
good place. The sisters are kind. I do not ever see them
hitting any of the girls. Am I the only one who is not
really a Catholic?

The dinner bell is ringing. We all go inside. The
dining room has many rectangular tables set up for six or

eight girls each. The cabbage soup smells delicious. So does the bread. We wait for Sister to lead us in grace and then we eat silently while Sister reads a story.

"Once upon a time there was a family of a mother, and a father, and a baby. The parents loved that baby intensely, especially because he was their only child. Even when the child was naughty, the parents could not bear to hit him. When he was seven years old, he became ill. The parents tried many medications and many physicians but nothing helped. The child died. Each week the parents went to the cemetery to leave flowers and prayers. One day they noticed the child's hand was sticking out of the grave. They buried it. The next time they visited, the hand was sticking out again. The priest they consulted advised them that the child felt guilty because he had been allowed to misbehave without proper punishment. Now he had to be punished even though he was dead. The parents had to hit that arm, and then it would stay buried."

I'm overwhelmed by the horror of such punishment. How can Jesus allow this? Wasn't this child baptized? Why didn't Jesus forgive him? There is so much that I do not understand here. I worry about my mom and dad. I must stop thinking about them. I must learn this Catholicism and appreciate my good luck in being allowed to live here, in this Catholic haven, even if only as Teresa. I must appreciate just being allowed to live.

10

The Warsaw Ghetto Uprising
Leonia, Spring 1943

I am alone now, without husband, without children, without any family. Rachel is in the convent, as safe a place as exists in this God-forsaken country, where I hope she is adjusting well. Even though I too am no longer inside the ghetto, I have no peace. My thoughts are constantly there, with my husband Joshua. The wall that separates us, the wall that separates those who may live from those who may not, is just a few short blocks from where I am working as a housekeeper. While shopping for food I pass even closer to it. During each day I hear the sound of shots reverberating from over that wall. At night I see my husband's fervent eyes looking for us, his face tired and charred and hungry. He is searching for us, Rachel and me. He wants to know that we are safe. I must find a way to let him know. I hope he is still alive, even as I know it cannot be for long.

Now that Rachel and I are on the Aryan side, he must be fighting with a more peaceful heart too. Now that we are gone, he can concentrate with purpose. Today, and whatever number of days might still be his to live, he will devote to only one goal. To help the battle; to exterminate, to kill, and to blow up as many Germans as possible before he himself is murdered. Were it not for

Rachel, I would have stayed there too. Many of our young soldiers are women. There is no difference between our sentiments and those of our men. We have all lost everyone we loved. There is no choice for us except to fight.

The Jewish uprising stuns the Germans. Our handful of untrained and starving young people, with nothing but homemade weapons and some captured guns, forces the Germans to bring in ever greater reinforcements. Thousands of Nazi troops equipped with massive firearms fight the resistance for weeks. They are no longer laughing at "the sheep so easily slaughtered." The Jews are holding out longer than anyone expected. It's an embarrassment for their "Reich." It must be finished.

The shots still ring out. Some of my people must still be alive. Maybe one of my brothers is there. I have no way of knowing if Joshua is among them. They might be hidden in a bunker or in a sewer. How long can they last?

The Germans choose April 19, the full moon of the first day of Passover, for their final assault. They set the ghetto on fire. Nothing is to be spared. Not a shred of it is to be left standing. They incinerate every building and every structure. Flames, red and purple and gold, leap up from the smoldering ruins. Silhouetted human shadows jump out of windows into the clouds of smoke whirling all around. The whoosh and the crackle of the fire consume the human cries, but nothing can keep out the smell of burning flesh that comes across with the spring breeze. The Jewish ghetto is turning to ashes.

We in the crowd are trying to protect our noses and our eyes from the polluted fumes. Acrid particles of scorched flesh permeate the air. It might be my husband's burned flesh that is mixed into those gases. It might be one of my brothers. It is certainly that of the last survivors.

My Joshua, dead or alive, is somewhere there. I'm standing on this side, among the throng of Polish multitude, just blocks away from the blistering flames. There had been no opportunity for me to find a way to contact my husband and to tell him that Rachel and I are all right. Now the flames have consumed even that small hope.

Crowds gather to watch the spectacle. All are revolted by the horror. Some cross themselves and pray silently. Some stare in disbelief at the barbarity. Some permit their eyes to show tears. Some turn away sickened, anxious to just get away from there. Some, like me, just numbly stand in silence.

I hear whispers among the throng.

"Mother of God, look what they are doing to the Jews."

"I don't like them, but they don't deserve this."

"Our poor, poor Warsaw."

A couple near me is apprehensive about their own future under this regime. They wonder if the fate of the Jews will be their fate too. No one likes the Germans, but I hear one man express satisfaction that at last the ghetto is finished and there will be no more "dirty Jews" to corrupt the glory of Poland.

How did Joshua die? I don't know. There is no picture of him, no stone to mark his life or death. How many Germans did he kill? Many, I hope. I only know that like the other young people of the Warsaw Ghetto Uprising, he died an unsung hero in the struggle of our people.

11

Don't Ask, Don't Tell
Rachel, Summer 1943

Dancing dust particles bounce in the early morning sunlight and come through our windows as if to say, "Hey, let's go out and play!" But playtime is rationed and takes second place to all the worries associated with the war. Today the lady from Warsaw will be coming to our convent to bring us important news about all that is happening around us here in Poland.

We take pains to prepare our best face for our guest. All our beds have been smoothed over. Our blankets, pillows, and personal items have been put away neatly in the boxes under our beds. We scrub our faces with a minimum of our rationed soap until they shine and hang up our individual towels that we always keep for a week. Most of us have braids. Mine are just long enough to tie together at the top of my head. We are ready and listening for the sound of the vehicle that will bring the lady from Warsaw.

Peace appears to reign on the gleaming, uncluttered surfaces of our dorm. A somber Virgin Mary regards us from one end of the room. Christ, drooping on the cross with the crown of thorns on his head, gazes down on us from the other end. The convent sisters tell us that the thorns are made by our sins. Good deeds, on the other hand, help to remove the thorns from his tortured head. I wonder *do good deeds by Jews count, too?*

From his vantage point high up near the ceiling, Christ can easily see the source of our problems. The German officers' quarters are just across the street. Their windows overlook the fence that surrounds the grounds of our convent. They can easily spy through the bare branches of our oak tree and into our own grounds and windows. German searchlights often focus on our building, especially on anyone coming or going. It's impossible to ignore the Germans' smothering presence.

Every morning we pray in the chapel to Jesus and to the Virgin Mary that they will exert their power to protect our families, our Poland, and ourselves. The chapel is an area of comfort, peace, and safety. I like being there. Our songs echo off the high walls and surely go straight up to heaven. The convent sisters assure us that our faith and prayers are heard and will be answered. Like most of the other girls, I pray fervently and hope the sisters are right.

The sisters float about like angels in milky white habits. Their appearance belies their difficult and dangerous responsibilities. They have no help here to take care of about twenty of us: They must clean this house, wash our clothes, make our meals, educate us, and see to all our other needs. But the most stressful part of their work is to protect themselves and us from the danger of suspicious German minds.

We are told that Zosia, the girl who sleeps just two beds away from my cot, gets a special hair wash every six or seven weeks to prevent lice, but that doesn't make sense. It does not happen to the rest of us. We think her hair is really red and that is why it gets dyed. I've heard some of the older girls whisper that only Jews have red hair. But I thought that I was the only Jewish girl here. It must have something to do with the suspicious Germans across the street.

Each of us girls has a story all her own, and we know that we must keep that story inside ourselves. Although our beds are quite close to one another, I hardly ever hear any late-night whispering. We do not share our backgrounds. I rarely hear anyone mention a mom, a dad, a sister, or a brother. Family visitors are very rare.

Zosia and I are especially sensitive because we do not want the sisters to send us away from here again. Once we were put onto a small wagon behind a horse and driven by Sister Angela to a convent outside Warsaw. It was a convent for the blind and deaf with a nice large yard and even some seesaw equipment. But nobody told us why we had to go there. We didn't know whether we had done something bad or why we were sent away.

After just a few weeks, Sister Angela came to bring us back again. As we were traveling back on a narrow dirt road through the forest area, we were stopped by four men who appeared without warning from the shadows of the trees. They were unkempt, with bloodshot eyes and red-blistered skin. Their hair and beards looked dirty; their clothing was tattered and grimy. We heard their gruff voices ask questions of Sister Angela who was sitting in the front. Her answers were muffled, but her voice was noticeably shaken and hesitant. She was frightened. We were too. When at last they let us go we heard their final forewarning, "If so much as a hair is missing from their heads, we will hold you personally responsible!" Sister Angela's face was ashen. But she didn't want to talk to us about it. The sisters in the convent were upset, too. They didn't seem happy to see us.

Something is wrong with Zosia and me.

We were told to be very careful, but we do not know what it was that we did wrong. It seems our very existence is a problem. If any stranger comes in—a delivery person, a messenger, or even a strange sister—we are told to disappear. Neither of us have ever been hit or treated unkindly by any of the sisters, but we are scared of something we cannot name. We spend a lot of time inside, behind closed doors. Sometime we just get behind an open door where we think we are unseen. Our hearts thump away as we seek solace from each other but only with our questioning eyes. I wonder, *Is she Jewish? Could she be Jewish too?* Neither of us dares to ask, nor would we admit even to each other, to being anything but good Catholics. We have both been baptized and we even have had communion. *So am I still Jewish anyway?*

Finally Sister introduces the lady from Warsaw, the visitor we have all been waiting for. She is probably the age of my mother. Her gray coat, matching hat, and gloves look elegant. She appears very important.

Courtesy requires us all to stand, curtsy, and then remain standing in front of our chairs until the lady tells us to sit. With a smile, she motions us to do so. She tells us about our courageous Polish partisans who are fighting against the Germans even with insufficient food and arms; about the terrible conditions that the Polish people must endure; about other countries, England and France, who are also fighting now. She admonishes us to continue to be brave. Regardless of our age, four or fourteen, we all must make do without complaint, eat every morsel of our meals, obey the sisters, and pray that the war ends soon.

All of us girls listen intently and politely as the lady continues. Lots of people are dying. We hear that the Germans are kidnapping people right from the streets and forcing them into labor. Nobody is safe. London, England, is under bombardment. But there is good news, too. America has joined the war. The lady believes that will help us win the war soon. It can't last much longer. But until then we must continue to be cautious and not arouse suspicion. We must be good Polish Catholic girls, and pray a lot: pray for our families (*did I still have one?*), pray for our people (*what people, Polish or Jewish?*), pray for the convent. Some of us are too young to remember a different time. Oh yes, we will all be very, very good girls to help the war effort.

I try to make sense out of these facts. Is this good news or bad news? Who is America? How far is England? What I really want to know is, what about the Jewish ghetto? Is my mother alive? Will I ever be able to see her or send her a message? I have not seen her in so very long! What about my dad? What happened to him after he helped my mom and me to escape over the ghetto wall? Is he still alive? When the war ends will I be Rachel or Teresa? Are the sins of Jews so bad?

Must not ask! Can't ask about my mother or my father because I am pretending to be an orphan. That means they are dead even if they are not. No mother and no father. Can't ask about the ghetto because I am pretending to be a Catholic. Catholics have no interest in the Jewish ghetto. The sisters never mention it. They think all Jews will go to hell anyway. Can't care about any of these things that really matter because I am not Rachel anymore. Rachel Szyfka the Jewish girl may be

*burning with curiosity, but Teresa Kurek, a Polish orphan, must
appear calm. She has no questions.*

A part of me spirits itself across the room and
watches the rest of the session like a discreet ghost. I take
the thoughts that are choking me and leave behind a
calm Teresa Kurek. There she is, a good, innocent little
Polish orphan with a clean face and nicely combed pig-
tails fastened on top of her head, politely listening to the
fine lady from Warsaw. Teresa has no past. She tries to
understand about London and America, but her mind is
just blank. This is okay for Teresa, but no help to me. I
block out the session and leave Teresa with the proper
Aryan mask covering her blank mind.

My hidden self searches the faces of the other girls
for clues. There are none that I can understand. Each
mask is just that. Each is attached to an equally unread-
able body. We do as the sisters tell us. We play together,
we pray together, we eat together, and we even laugh at
silly jokes together. We climb the tree in the yard and
jump rope together. Sometimes we make wreaths for our
hair out of leaves held together with pine needles. But
our togetherness is only on the surface. I know I cannot
communicate what is most important in my heart.

I know I must not reveal my anxiety to any of the
other girls, nor to the sisters either. They probably all
think Jews are wicked and deserve all this because they
killed Christ. They think Jews are dirty and crude and
that their souls will surely go to hell. Sister Bernarda said
that even good Jews cannot go to heaven because they do
not accept Jesus. I dare not think about my family. If they
are dead, are they already burning in hell? What about
the Christians who are doing all this killing? Can God be
so unfair?

I force my mind to recede to a tiny secret space, which I lock tight. These are not useful thoughts. I can think them only in my secret place. Now I must rejoin Teresa. I must make sure no one suspects that I am not really she. She and I must continue this farce and never, never ask or tell.

12

Those Darned Socks
Rachel, Early Winter 1943

I watch as Sister Archangela slips my dirty sock over her narrow hand. The sleeve of her cream-white habit falls to her elbow. Her slender twenty-some-year-old arm shows signs of red patches and rough skin, a marked contrast to the smooth fabric. But her face emanates a sense of peace, order, and cleanliness. Grace and good manners are just a part of her. Never once does she grimace or hold her nostrils to shut out the smell of those stinky socks only inches away from her aquiline nose.

The task at hand is to darn the hole in the sock. The threaded needle is waiting, waiting to patch the holes that World War II created in my socks, just as it had in the lives and the economy of occupied Poland. First, Sister explains, the hole has to be completely opened, not sewn together, so that the contour of the sock will stay the same, and its size will not shrink. The trick is to open your thumb and forefinger so as to create a foundation for darning, while at the same time holding the rest of the sock taut with your remaining fingers. If your hand is too small, you can also use a mushroom-shaped darning cup, but we do not have enough of those. The important thing is to be able to maintain the integrity of the original shape of the sock. "Don't ever forget," she kids us half seriously, "that even a sock should have integrity."

Sister Archangela and every one of us kids take this job very seriously. Sister knows that these socks are all we have to keep our feet warm through the bitter Polish winter. She also knows that many of us do not have an extra pair. Any mending or cleaning has to be done overnight. She can't do it all by herself. All of us, even almost-seven-year-old girls like myself, have to help.

There are quite a few of us for the sisters to worry about. All those socks and no washing machine. First the water has to be heated in the kitchen. Then the laundry is done by hand over washing boards and hung by the heater. Hopefully it will be dry for the next day. Most of our garments are washed once a week, but our socks cannot wait that long. Hard wear combined with dirt and sweat makes them a constant challenge.

This is especially true because the sisters believe in long walks, plenty of exercise, and lots of fresh air. It is their rationalization that since they cannot provide us with good nutrition, proper educational material, or adequate warm garments, at least we will get plenty of good, fresh, cold Polish air. It is free and even the Nazis have not been able to find a way to ration it.

Our walks are often taken in the late afternoon. By then the midday dinner is already done. If our clothes, shoes, and socks get wet in the snow, we don't have to worry about what to wear when we come back. After we eat supper, the evening is short. Dusk comes early and we go to bed. If we are lucky, our shoes and socks have time to dry overnight—after the socks are darned and washed, of course.

Rochelle Dreeben

I look forward to our darning sessions. Sister sits down with just a few of us in a group that is small enough for her to be able to supervise carefully. Once we are all settled in, she brings out her precious basket of darning equipment. Each piece of thread is meted out thoughtfully. Each needle is tracked. Only Sister herself is allowed to touch the treasured basket. When it is not being used, only she knows where it is stored.

Darning requires that the sock, like a good book, be held about fifteen inches from the face. Most of us kids are not as elegantly disciplined as Sister Archangela. "Phew!" We hold our noses and make faces as the daunting smells traverse the room. Sister will not have any of it.

"Pay attention!" she commands. There is no meanness in her words.

"Don't forget to give your darning a solid base in the area around the hole. If you do not, your work will not hold." Holding one of the socks she demonstrates the right method. "Start with the surrounding area, like this, so that the mending has something to sit on. Then weave the thread back and forth horizontally across the hole. When that is done you must weave the vertical thread between the horizontal lines. You must do it without making a knot at the end of your thread, or your feet will not be happy."

Sister positions my sock on my hand and gives me a threaded needle. She watches vigilantly while I make my first stitch. "Good," she encourages, and guides me to go across the hole, and a little bit further, and then to return, back and forth, again and again, keeping the distances even. It's a real challenge.

There is neither time nor thread to be wasted. It is an important job, and I look forward to doing it well. As I get better and my socks get worse, there is not only the simple hole, but also the compound hole that needs darning. The wearing out of an already darned area creates the compound hole. Keeping the whole thing as smooth as possible is the goal. I have experienced the truth of what Sister is trying to teach us. Sloppy darning is sure to make my feet very sore the next day.

Sometimes the darning session is made especially pleasant by stories recounted by Sister or read by one of the older girls. Other times it is an opportunity to talk or to sing. But the best part comes from the feeling of pride. A well-darned hole is a worthy accomplishment. It might earn a flattering remark from Sister. It is sort of like a medal on the heel of your foot. At the very least it is very satisfying to be able to wear it comfortably the next day.

In mid-December of 1943, Sister detains me after everyone else is excused. "You're extremely lucky," she tells me. "You will have the chance to spend Christmas with a wonderful family. Mr. and Mrs. Chrabioski have invited you to be their guest in their beautiful home for the whole week of Christmas."

I have no idea what to expect. I have never been a "guest" in someone's home. The sisters assure me that it will be a wonderful experience and all I have to do is behave properly, as of course I will.

The house of the Chrabioskis sits all by itself on the outskirts of Warsaw. It has so many rooms that I am allowed to sleep in one all by myself. Besides the bed, there is a chest of drawers with two wonderful things I had not seen in years: a good-sized mirror and a large chiming clock, which sits on its own three feet just under the mirror. They make an elegant pair. Even though there are no other children in the house, I am never bored for an instant. Whenever I pass that mirror, I study my face sneakily. At the moment it is a rather square face, dominated by nice eyes and a too-wide grin. Two light-brown braids come down just behind my ears. Today Mrs. Chrabioska (in Polish, all female names end in "a") has tied each of them with a shiny pink bow. Sometimes she puts my braids up on my head like a crown with a special clasp. I feel like a princess. Before bedtime in the evening, when no one is looking, I let my hair loose and admire all the waves left from the braids. I wish they were blonde and naturally curly. Would I have been reprimanded if the sisters saw me primping like that? I have seen Mrs. Chrabioska sit in front of the mirror and fuss with her makeup for quite a while. She does not think it is bad.

I love to listen to the tick-tock of the clock on my dresser and watch that sweeping second hand point to all the Roman numerals. Mrs. Chrabioska teaches me how to make sense of them and how to tell time. Sister Ena explained it in the convent, but I didn't really understand it until now, when I have a real clock in my own room. I practice at every opportunity. "Is it a quarter of two now?" I check the hour for the fifteenth time today. She looks at me with an amused grin and nods her head. I check her expression but there is no indication that I'm annoying her.

When not verifying the time of day, Mrs. Chrabioska and I make Christmas ornaments out of paper and matchboxes and strings and paint. We make long ribbons out of colored paper. I love the red ones. We make little girl figures and angel figures with glued-on silver wings. I feel somewhat experienced because at the convent, too, we have been making paper chains and boxes with glued-on colored hair from scrap material or string. They are lots of fun to make and I relish every bit of it. Just about when I think that our box of handmade stuff is perfect, Mrs. Chrabioska brings out a box of very special and delicate ornaments. Some glisten with gold or shimmering red lacquer. As she unwraps each ornament from its tissue, she tells me its history. "This one is from my grandparents, from the time Poland was under Russian occupation. They are all beautifully painted. If you take off the head of the doll, there is another one inside just a little bit smaller." She shows me how to do it and then lets me do it myself. When I finish, there are ten dolls around the Christmas tree. Each is just a bit smaller than the previous one. Each one's costume is hand-painted in vibrant colors. "That silvery angel is from a trip we took to Paris before the war." She never questions me about my background. Does she know?

We hang the special ornaments along with our handmade ones to get just the right balance of colors and shapes. Then we stand back to consider the effect, add others, and stand back again. The tree has to have that magical charm of fairylike sparkle and light. I am careful, of course, and very aware of the trust I am given to handle these delicate treasures. There is always just one more thing to do to make it perfect, and then another thing to make it even better. Making it beautiful is work that I love.

Christmas morning there is a box for me. It is my very first ever Christmas present. I open it slowly, savoring every moment. First, off comes the string of red wool, which I carefully wind for future use; then comes the paper, which I also fold and save; and finally I open the box. There, in majestic splendor on delicate white tissue, is a pair of red wool socks. Just like the color of the wool bow that decorated the gift box itself. Mrs. Chrabioska knitted them just for me. They are perfect, without a single hole and without any darned area either. They come all the way up to my knees, where they have fuzzy pom-poms that hang on the side for decoration. There is plenty of room at the toes for my feet to grow. I put my hands in the socks and absorb their fuzzy warmth. I am so lucky. I will cherish them forever. What a wonderful Christmas.

When I go back to the convent, I stash my treasured socks in my box under my bed. Sometimes I take them out to sleep with me. Just touching those soft red fuzzy pom-poms gives me a feeling of great wealth and security. These precious socks have to be saved for only the most special occasion. They should never be marred by a stinking hole. I continue to wear and darn the old socks so as to preserve the new ones.

(The sisters do not tell me that the Chrabioskis are considering me for adoption. I have no idea that Sister Bernarda tells my mother about it, expecting approval. Instead my mother is horrified. She responds that without me she has no reason to live. Sister understands. The adoption proceedings are stopped.)

Shortly thereafter, the Germans force us out of our convent home. They want to use it for their own Nazi officers' quarters. The move is hasty and disorganized; we have almost no advance notice. The sisters divide us into smaller groups that can be accommodated more easily in other convents or schools. We are shifted from one place to another until a group of us finally arrives in Koslo. Many things disappear. No one knows where Sister Archangela's darning basket is. No one knows where my never-yet-worn, never-darned, beautiful red wool socks are.

13

Koslo*
Rachel 1944–1945

Neither the winter nor the Nazis are ready to concede defeat in these early months of 1944. Both relentlessly pursue their goals, chilling this land and destroying both humanity and humaneness. But the winter's power is waning. Here and there a crocus springs out of the snow; an early bird's shadow is seen gliding over the vast whiteness. The fresh perfume of spring insinuates itself into the wet, chilling wind. Longer and brighter days are dawning.

After the Germans had forced us to leave our convent, we spent a couple of days at another convent school and a couple of days at a home for the blind before about eighteen of us finally settled here in Koslo. It's a small farm village roughly 80 miles south of Warsaw. Our new home is a large barn-like structure. In fact, it is a barn.

It has been a tough winter for all of us, and for our hard-working sisters who had to make this place livable. Somehow they put it together, even though we lack elemental comforts. One side of the large room is a sleeping area with our straw mattresses; on the other side are a few school desks. There are some towels, a few

*Some of the stories in this chapter were related to me by sister Ena, long after war.

washbasins. There are three chamber pots behind a curtain. No cleaning tools, no toys, no books, no educational supplies. A wood stove that requires a lot of tending sits in the middle of the room and adds more light than heat. It is the only shelter we have and we are lucky to have it.

We are a motley bunch of girls between four and twelve years old and a few very good, very kind, and very brave sisters. We even have one boy for a short while. Jedrus is about five or six years old. He was wounded in his shoulder and leg. The sisters call him Warsaw's youngest resistance fighter. He is with us only briefly. The sisters tell us he was taken to a different convent.

Manya, one of the girls, was wounded too. She has no visible scars, but her hurts are deep and never quite heal. She and her father came to us while we were still in the Warsaw convent. He had been shot. The sisters put him in the basement to hide him from prying eyes and tried to care for him. Manya would not leave him for a moment. She slept with him and looked only at him. When the sisters found him dead, she was still holding his hand. It was difficult to tear Manya away from his body. For a long time she brooded and cried and refused to eat or to join any activity. Eventually she transferred her attachment to the sisters and followed them everywhere like a devoted puppy.

Basia and Jadzia's mom had left them at our convent with a note saying, "Here you have the beggar children of Warsaw." They were bony, wretched, and ravenously hungry. They were clothed in rags that were held together with pins and were so filthy that the sisters burned even the straw where the girls slept their first night. Parts of their faces had patches of white skin. The sisters told us they were caused by extreme cold. One of the sisters wrapped the girls in her own garments.

Fortunately, just around that time our convent acquired a large piece of flannel. The sisters set about making all of us badly needed garments. They sewed new uniforms, underpants, shirts, and tunics for us, all identical in navy blue with white stripes. We thought we were in the height of fashion design.

Sister Ena tells of a time when little Basia appeared to be showing off. "I saw the Polish Eagle," she stated.

"How?" asked Sister Ena, knowing that any Polish symbol of independence is forbidden. "Perhaps it was a pigeon?"

"No. It was a small child. The Germans cut it with a sword and threw it in the air. The child was waving its arms. The Germans laughed and said, 'There, now you have a Polish Eagle.'"

The townspeople of Koslo are our benefactors, especially one of our sisters' natural siblings who lives here. Thanks to their generosity, we receive potatoes, cabbage, and whatever else they can spare. It is insufficient for health, but good enough for survival. For Easter they outdo themselves and bring us a treasure; enough eggs to allow everyone of us to have a whole one. We all look forward to this special treat, and many of us even write our names on our very own egg. We are anxious to go out and be done with our daily walk so we can enjoy our egg-supper.

All except Irka, who is excused from walking because she constantly complains that her legs hurt. There is nothing to her except a pair of black shiny eyes and a huge stomach balanced on spider legs. Always hungry.

Likes to be all by herself. When the rest of us come back from our walk, smiling and happy in anticipation of our treat, we find an unwelcome surprise. All the eggs have disappeared. Rats? Cats? No. Irka is the only one home. She confesses. Seventeen eggs and she does not even get sick, not even a stomachache! The sisters make her say she is sorry to all of us, but they do not punish her. She keeps to herself for the next couple of days. That was her way even before.

Easter brings other surprises. Our sisters are able to get hold of some better-grade fabric that was permitted into the country only because it was really meant for some *volksdeutsch* family (ethnic Germans living abroad). It included percale and flannel. Some townspeople grumble about it being too fine for just orphans, but we get it anyway. Our sisters work hard to make each of us our own towel marked with our own name, a change of underwear, a dress, and best of all, a bed sheet. What luxury to have real, smooth, all-cotton sheets!

The sisters try to teach us what they can remember and to keep us occupied as well. Since some girls are only four years old and others are as old as twelve, it is a difficult task. They tell us stories, especially about Polish history and its heroes. Sister Angela teaches geography and singing. In secret we bastardize the Polish anthem by replacing the original words with "We will yet see Hitler hang upside-down after he gets cholera" (a Polish curse as well as the disease). It is all forbidden so we think we are very clever. Someone from town is kind enough to bring us some little chalkboards. We use them to practice letters. Someone else donates a few notebooks and pencils. I learn the alphabet and am able to understand the organization of letters into words. Koslo is beginning to feel comfortable, like home! And thank goodness it's almost spring.

Going to church is difficult because it is a long way away and located in a drafty wooden building. Those who can walk the distance need some extra clothes, so we borrow anything that is not in use by those who are not going. Father Kulejewski is our friend as well as our protector. He is a jovial man who always makes us feel welcome. Sometimes he walks us part of the way home after church and even suggests that we take tin cups with us. If we see a cow, we run up to the owner and hopefully get treated to warm, creamy milk straight from the udder. We love our yummy white whiskers. The priest thanks the farmer profusely and compliments and blesses him. It's a super treat. We are very grateful and very happy.

As the snow thaws, the mood in our cluster becomes more positive. The sisters tell us the war will be over soon, that the Germans are beginning to retreat, going westward to their own country. We hear comments that the arrogance on their faces is fading, that their uniforms are becoming shabbier.

A short time later we begin to see different soldiers, in even shabbier uniforms. They are the soldiers of the Red army, who are marching in from the east. They too have haggard, frozen faces above their raised collars. They sing of victory as they drag their legs through the middle of the fields, exhausted, gray, needing sleep.

Now and then a parent or a family member comes to claim one of us scrawny, bowlegged kids. Will I be one of them? Will my mom, if she is even alive, find me or even want me?

14

A Devout Christian Maid
Leonia, 1943–1944

Shortly after Sister Bernarda arranged for Rachel to be in the convent, I made a promise to her that should we survive, I would never attempt to dissuade Rachel from practicing Catholicism. I intend to keep that promise. It is a small price to pay for my daughter's life. Now that Rachel is safe and I am situated working for Pani Kwiatowska, Sister has come for a visit and she is trying to make me a convert as well. I listen, but really I must resist.

My own soul will have to deal with whatever God has in store for it. I cannot in good conscience promise Sister that I too will become a Catholic, not even though I want to please this extraordinary woman. Not even when she appeals to me through my daughter by saying that Rachel—I mean Teresa—too is concerned about my afterlife, and wants to be assured that my soul will get to heaven, just like hers.

If it were her religion that made Sister such a noble-minded human being, then pursuing that faith would be tempting. But of course she is a rare individual. Many other Christians and even the Catholic Church itself have been propagating anti-Semitism for generations. The Nazis, too, consider themselves Christians.

"Come, let me baptize you." Sister encourages as her hands hold the big cross on the chain around her neck.

"Sister, if I do it now, it will be only because I want you to save me—I mean save my life here on earth. If I do it after the war, it will be an honest conversion."

Sister hugs me. "You know, there are not many Jews as honorable as you. You see, I don't particularly like Jews, but I do want to save them. Especially I want to save their souls for eternity."

Even though Sister fails to make a sincere convert out of me, we both know that my appearance cannot be questionable. I must have the necessary icons commonly worn by Polish Catholics. She reaches into one of her enormous pockets and produces a tin chain with the Virgin Mary and a crucified Jesus attached to it. These she fastens around my neck. She also gives me a book of prayers and a rosary. I will take good care of them. They are my security. They are always in my hands or in my purse. Of course I agree that I will go to church every Sunday. There is peace in church, also beautiful music, tranquility, and a measure of temporary safety. On occasion, when my burdens overwhelm me, I am tempted to even go to confession and so as to relieve my burdens. I know it could be dangerous or even a trap, so I would need to guard my words. I can't quite trust the priest's conscience and his vow of silence.

I have been working here for a couple of months now. Pani Kwiatowska is a dressmaker specializing in the alteration of furs. It is my duty to do the cleaning and cooking for her. But most of my time is devoted to the sewing and the alterations of her customers' garments. Often the fancy fur brought in by a patron appears to be very valuable, much more expensive than one would expect her to be able to afford. "Oh, my husband just gave it to me, for my birthday" the lady might volunteer. Only later, while resizing the fur, I recognize a Jewish name inside the garment. I don't know how she got it, but I do know why it needs alteration.

Of course I never say anything. I have my suspicions and Pani Kwiatowska has hers. Often she looks at me with a questioning expression. She may be testing me when she says, "Those people are certainly odd and dirty." Of course I know she is referring to Jews, and I'm forced to nod in agreement. I must not utter so much as a phrase of kindness or tolerance. An expression of humaneness could be a giveaway. I can display only indignation. But at night, when I try to fall asleep on my cot in the small alcove off the kitchen, I wonder how I can guard against calling out a Jewish name, a Jewish word, a Jewish anguish.

Once, as I am cooking, she observes, "You cut onions like a Jewess." Really! I can't imagine how I cut onions in any unusual way. We really do not trust each other, but I need the job and she is reluctant to rid herself of a good worker.

In the same building where Pani Kwiatowska lives, there are rumors that a family is hiding a Jewish child. It is probably the youngster that I like to watch as she plays in the courtyard. The little girl looks absolutely Polish. She is about the same age as my own Rachel. Her skin is light and she has dirty blond braids. Gossip has it that the parents gave this Polish family a sum of money to hide her, but that the relatives of the family are jealous and threaten to report her unless they too are bribed.

Someone must have squealed. Returning from an errand, I find the building surrounded by Nazi officers.

The street is barricaded. No one is allowed in or out while the Nazis are searching. When I ask the people gathered on the street what is going on, they explain that the Germans are looking for that child. I have not seen her here for a while. I believe she has been moved to another hiding place, somewhere in the country. Thank God that this one tragedy has been averted. It could have been the end, not only for the child but for that good family as well.

When I finally gain entry to Pani Kwiatowska's apartment and ask, "What happened?" she answers sarcastically, "As if you did not know!" Next day I leave for an errand. I never return.

After several such positions, I wind up with the Holzmans. They are of German extraction and therefore less apt to notice the difference between a Polish Jew and a Polish Aryan. Mr. Holzman is an engineer working for the German war effort, so they are entitled to special privileges, such as a beautiful home near the Łazienki Park of Warsaw, extra food rations, and so on. A woman comes there daily to deliver milk. She hears me singing hymns to myself and is so impressed with my religious zeal that she tries to persuade me to take a job at a priest's house. But I am content to stay where the work is hard but where I am not suspected of being anything other than an uneducated, lower-class Polish peasant. The deception is working and the war may be coming to an end.

15

It's Me or the *Hunt*
Leonia, Winter 1944

I hear that first low growl even before I turn my steps onto the path. As I get closer, the sound becomes more menacing. It is followed by a bark that shatters my nerves. It states, "I am big and powerful and I don't want you here!" I want to turn and run, but No! I've overcome far greater dangers than a dog. I will not be cowed by a bark. A mahogany door opens to reveal a tall, dark-haired woman holding back a wolf. Between the animal's parted lips hangs a dark red tongue flanked by long fangs. The dog's ears, white inside and framed in black, stand up sharply. Its eyes glare at me.

"You must be Basia," the lady greets me, then orders, "Fritz, sit!" The knuckles on her hands stand out as she strains to keep control of Fritz's leash. "Don't be afraid of him, he is a wonderful dog once he gets to know you," she assures me. Fritz continues his low-pitched growling.

This is to be my fourth housekeeping job since I assumed the identity of an Aryan maid. I left several other jobs because I was afraid someone suspected me of being Jewish. In the last place I worked, the lady liked to watch me work, while she gossiped and insinuated dark meanings, "The police were here this morning while you were at the market. I wonder what they were looking for?" "Strange that a pretty girl like you has never been married. Where is your family? Don't they care about you?"

When Sister Bernarda arranged this new job, she told me that I might actually be safer with the Holzmans because they are *Volksdeutsche* and probably not as intuitive in noticing the difference between a Pole and a Jew. I set out to like them and even Fritz if possible.

This house is located near Łazienki Park, just on the southern edge of Warsaw. Before the war I spent delightful afternoons here, both as a child and later as a mother. My husband, my baby Rachel, and I enjoyed strolling among the centuries-old trees imported from all over the world. The white castle in the center, surrounded by a man-made lake that reflects its neoclassical lines, provides stillness and grace. Pheasants roam freely, and in the spring the males show off their plumage as they do their beautiful courting dance. On Sundays, weather permitting, Chopin concerts are played there outdoors. Those are wonderful. Even the birds stop to listen. It has been at least four years since I was there last.

Mrs. Holzman is wearing a navy blue dress covered almost completely by an apron of similar color. She explains my duties in Polish but with a twinge of German accent. First thing in the morning before anyone in the family is up, I'm to bring coal from the basement and light the fireplaces; set the table; make the coffee; put out the bread, butter, and so forth, and take Fritz for his morning walk. Mrs. Holzman suggests that I take Fritz at least as far as Łazienki Park, which is about two kilometers away. Fritz and I should be back by seven thirty so that I can help with making the eggs, sausage, or cooked cereal for herself, her husband, and their twelve-year-old son, Hans.

She demands hard work but she is fair. She is well aware that even though the house is modest in size, there is no end to the cleaning. Fritz sheds everywhere, and his fur is constantly on the carpets and furniture—the brown and black hair deposited in single strands and the white, down-soft undercoat in clumps. It is there after the morning cleaning and shopping at the market for the day's dinner. It is there after the washing and the cooking. It is especially there when we come back from outside and Fritz gives himself a healthy shake. His fur and frozen water droplets fly all over.

Fritz must have ever-fresh water, and his food has to be prepared just as though he were another person in the family. It is important that he be brushed frequently so that his coat is shiny and the Holzmans can show him off with pride. Mrs. Holzman lets me know that even though that is their son's job, most of it will probably fall to me. Hans is supposed to walk with the dog and me for the first two weeks, but being a German nearing his teens, Hans is not pleased to walk with a Polish maid. He asks me to walk behind him "so as not to upset the dog," and persuades his parents to let me do it by myself after just two days.

Simply putting the leash on Fritz's powerful neck sets both my and Fritz's nerves on edge. This leash is a handsome piece of strong, soft leather engraved with Fritz's name. Like every other piece of the well-maintained furniture and equipment in the house, it has to be waxed and polished. It hangs on its own hook right next to Hans's coat.

Mrs. Holzman practices her piano playing frequently. She has a nice singing voice too. She is also proud of her housekeeping. Every piece of clothing in this home has to be properly washed, starched, ironed, and hung on its own hanger. There is a place and time for everything. Proper manners are important too for greeting, for eating, even for enjoyment. Occasionally I hear properly cultivated laughter and proper German music coming from the living room where Mrs. Holzman, properly attired, entertains her guests. Fritz is usually there too, and he never growls or barks.

Everyone can see the love and respect that Fritz and Mrs. Holzman have for each other. Her blue Aryan eyes look into his black canine ones with complete trust. When her hand slowly slides over his thick, shiny coat or under his ears, he makes unmistakable sounds of satisfaction. She is the only one for whom he turns over to be fondled under his thick neck and on his soft underside. And his place to sleep is right at the side of her bed. Their loyalty to each other is as clear as the windows that I have to wash whenever he paws them, jumping with excitement to see her coming back home. But when he turns to look at me, there is what appears to be hatred in those eyes. Even though I feed him and walk him, he continues to watch me with distrust.

The Holzmans eat supper promptly at seven. After I serve them and Fritz, who also eats in the dining room, I am given time to eat my own meal in the kitchen. I must give credit to Mrs. Holzman for insisting that her son should never bother me while I am eating. I am not to be disturbed. I try to take advantage of this time to rest somewhat, because I know that immediately after doing the dishes, I still have to face that final walk with Fritz. He weighs almost as much as I do, and he is infinitely stronger. His coat is thick with an extra under-layer for winter. It is much warmer and much better fitting than mine. He loves the snow and even the ice. He pulls to keep going while I freeze and strain to keep my balance. He is secure on those four well-padded paws, but the leather on the soles of my shoes is thin and slippery.

Fritz and I never become friends. Even after a year he barely tolerates me and makes no pretense about it. Mrs. Holzman is puzzled. "I just don't understand why he dislikes you, of all people! You do so much for him and he is such a loving animal. All our friends are impressed with Fritz."

"Well, I guess he resents me because I force him to go home when he wants to walk further." In my head I think, *Damn him! I hate this German shepherd. He probably knows I'm Jewish, but thank God he can't talk. This* Hunt *is like a prince here, and I feel like his slave. He has the right to live and I do not.*

God, I pray as I get up from a nasty fall during one particularly cold evening walk, *give me a sign. Show me that after all this misery I will see the end of the Germans; that I will survive this war and this* Hunt. *God, give me a sign! Make this* Hunt *die as a signal to me that I will live and be reunited with Rachel.*

A few weeks later Fritz gets sick. There is something wrong with his stomach. Trips from one veterinarian to another fail to find the problem. As directed, I make him special chicken soup and meat that is well cooked. Sometimes Mrs. Holzman checks it to make sure there are no bones. She stays home often now, and caresses him, and talks to him while I clean up the messes that occur when his bowels do not work properly. Mrs. Holzman prays vehemently, and I pray too, though not for the same result. My prayers seem to have greater strength than hers. Fritz keeps getting worse. *Perhaps it is some poison he picked up on some walk? Did I ever see him eat anything suspect?* I really did not. It is an act of God. Fritz dies.

The Holzmans mourn and mourn. I try to be sad too, but my chores are much easier now. After dinner I rest and even have time to read about the course of the war. It seems to be coming to a fortuitous end. Perhaps there is a God! I am beginning to have faith that there is integrity in his sign to me. After all, Fritz died, I am still alive, and Yes! I dare to believe that I will survive not only Fritz but the war as well!

16

Polish Revolt
Leonia, Winter 1944

On every rubble-filled street I see men and women, young and old, walking around with their lips pursed and their teeth clenched. Their eyes dart with hatred and resentment toward the soldiers relaxing just across the river. It's the Red Army. They are so close. They are easily visible to the naked eye. They do not lift so much as a grenade to help the Polish revolt against the Germans. How can they watch the Poles being crushed by German bombers and continue to sit idle? So many thousands have already died! Everyone's enraged. One hears the same remarks all around, "Those rotten Red bastards, they're no better than the Nazis. Cholera should take them all!"

I sympathize with the Poles, and certainly wish them victory over the Nazis. Yet I wonder if any of them remember when it was the Jewish uprising begging for Polish help. It was just a year ago. We were begging the Poles for help against our common enemy. Almost none came. I understand their frustration. I remember how we felt when we knew that they were just watching our annihilation and the incineration of the ghetto. They simply sat there, just across that ghetto wall. My husband was there, and maybe some of my brothers too. As the ghetto was going up in flames, I stood among the Polish crowd just outside the wall and watched my history and my people turned into ashes. I stood there as an Aryan, outside of the ghetto wall, and I could not even allow myself to feel the full brunt of that tragedy. I just stood there mute and frozen. Now I can well understand the bitterness of the Polish resentment. For me it's something of a déjà vu; nonetheless I too wish the Russians would help.

I have not seen or heard from Rachel for almost two years. A couple of times I took a trolley to the convent and tried to look through the fence, but I saw her only once, briefly. She was playing with some of the other girls and appeared quiet. I could not hear anything above the usual street noise. Some time later Sister Bernarda told me that the Nazis had commandeered the whole convent building for their own use, so all the children and the sisters had had to be moved. She did not tell me where they had gone. But I know they are out of this city and safer than they would have been here. The Germans are punishing the revolt by bombing Warsaw unmercifully.

Even the Holzmans's house has been hit and damaged. They decide to abandon what is left of it and to go to Germany. They suggest that I can stay with one of their friends for a couple of days while I decide what to do. But soon their friends also decide to leave. They tell me that I am welcome to stay in their house and to help myself to anything they leave. For about two days I remain there, then I attempt to contact Sister Bernarda to help me resolve what to do next. Before I leave the house I check around to see if there are some clothes or boots that would be useful to me. I do find a long wool sweater and a good warm coat. I am very glad to have those on my back when I get caught in a German raid.

The German war effort is faltering and the Germans need more slaves to help with the manufacture of their war needs. Everybody is a potential target. Even if you have papers to verify that you are an Aryan, you are no longer safe. They aren't even looking at papers. They just grab people off the streets. Now that they have murdered the Jewish slave labor, they need Poles to do those tasks.

I was hoping to find a telephone or some way to contact Sister, but just as soon as I turn a corner into the next street I see the trap. It's too late to get out. A soldier standing five feet away from me is pointing his gun and directing me into an open truck idling noisily in the middle of the street. "*Schnell, schnell!*" he yells, thrusting daggers of hatred at me with his eyes. I steel myself to ignore his humiliating commands as he pushes me toward the doors. Just like the others I do as he says.

The truck is already filled with other captives, most of them women. Some are trying to appeal to his humaneness: "My children have no one else; have mercy on them." "Let me go! I'm a doctor and I must be in the hospital." One is sobbing while telling the guard that she left a young child home alone. His expression never changes. He speaks no Polish or doesn't care. His job is to stand ready to shoot anyone attempting flight. The truck takes off toward the railroad station.

We are loaded onto an old and dirty passenger car. At least it has seats and I am lucky enough to get one. By comparison to the sealed, windowless cattle cars used for my people, this is luxury, but my fellow passengers despair just the same. "Jesus, Maria, they do with us the same as they did with the Jews. Are they taking us for work or to murder us? Where are we going?" I hear terrified whispers. There are cries of fear all around. The woman with the toddler is sobbing hysterically. The train is gaining speed.

The woman sitting next to me is a well-dressed, pleasant-looking person. She and I quickly establish a rapport. Her name is Marzena Bielanska. She tells me she is a lawyer. Her husband is either dead or a prisoner. She too is in her thirties and looks pretty fit. We agree that we must try to escape at the very first opportunity. We both know the trains are in bad shape and often have to stop for emergency repairs. If that occurs, we must force the door open or break a window and run for it. It is our only chance.

"So what do you think, shall we try to escape together?"

"Yes, I think so—but be prepared to dodge bullets because they will shoot, you know. Are we in agreement that if the train starts to slow down we spring at once, ready to run?"

She knows. She is smart. She agrees and cautions me, "Remember that if we get a chance, we must run together but at least six feet apart. That way, we will make a more difficult target. If one of us gets hit, the other must continue."

Sure enough, less than an hour out of Warsaw the train grinds to a screeching halt. We are in the middle of a farm area. Guards holler that if anybody moves they will be killed. Nonetheless doors are forced open. Some jump out of windows. People run every which way. Bullets ring out. Screams follow. Some fall wounded and continue to crawl away. Some are killed. My newfound friend and I do not even look around as we run to get as far from the carnage as possible. Marzena's caution proves providential. A bullet whizzes by between us and hits the ground just feet ahead. We keep running, running until we reach an area of woods. We both flop down behind the trunk of an old oak.

For a few moments we just breathe hard, neither of us able to talk. Finally we stand up and look around. It's a farm area, fields and forests that are totally unfamiliar to me. My friend looks around with a totally different reaction. Her eyes light up. She begins to laugh and shake her head. Is she crazy or is this just nervous relief? Finally she explains, "It's amazing. How funny that the Germans brought me here of all places. I love this place. In fact, I have been hoping to get out of Warsaw and come here, but couldn't because as you know all the trains had been requisitioned for the Germans. Basia, I can't believe how lucky we are. I know this place like my own backyard. We are in Rawa Mazowietska, and I own a villa just a few kilometers from here. My mother lives there now. You are welcome to stay with us and I'm sure you can find a job there, too."

Marzena's villa turns out to be an eight-room summerhouse. Her mother, Pani Bielanska, greets us with surprise and warmth. She scurries to get us some freshly made cabbage soup and bread. It is the staple here, as it is everywhere in Poland. I have had nothing to eat this day and I savor every spoonful. The freshness of the vegetables makes this a most delicious treat, especially because fresh produce is almost impossible to get in Warsaw.

Marzena will live upstairs with her mother. They offer me a room on the ground floor. They are confident that I am a fine person, caught like themselves in unfortunate circumstances. Some other Warsaw exiles are already living in a couple of the downstairs rooms. One of them mentions that the local bakery needs some help and I can probably work there if I wish. I'm grateful for their hospitality and the work they arrange for me. My job in the local bakery means washing dishes, kneading dough, and serving customers when needed. This is a twelve-hour-a-day job, six days a week. I get a small stipend and, just as importantly, some of the unsold bread, which is much appreciated by my new family of exiles. On Sundays we all go to church. It's a good place and we all like the priest. Afterwards we occasionally share a meal.

One day I open the door and find a woman and a child begging for any space. They are visibly exhausted and desperate. I can see Marzena wants to help them, but there are no more rooms. She looks at me in a quandary. I'm the only person there with a room all to myself. Of course I don't mind sharing my room. I do not spend much time there anyway. The job in the bakery keeps me very busy and by the time I get home I am so tired that I can sleep anywhere. It is just what she wants to hear!

"Such a good Christian you are!" Pani Bielanska has a great big smile of approval for me. She has a good soul and is happy to accommodate yet another needy woman and her child. Sometimes when I come in late at night and see the little girl sleeping, I wonder where my own child is sleeping these days.

One of the local peasants has been watching me suspiciously. He comes into the bakery and accuses me of being Jewish. By now I have become an accomplished actress. I know my lines and play them convincingly. "May cholera strike you, you bastard! How dare you call me a rotten Jew. Let Mary, mother of Christ, protect me from snakes like you!" I clasp the necklace holding the "virgin" and cross myself. Confused, he backs down, at least temporarily.

But I have another problem. I have no idea how to rid myself of the Ukrainian farm boy who wants to become my lover. As an unmarried maiden I am fair game, and he is not giving up. He brings me gifts of cheap jewelry and offers himself on any terms. How about if he rents a room so we can have a private love nest? When I come and go to work, he follows me, pestering and propositioning me. I am frightened. Who can help me? The only person I can appeal to is our priest. He is most sympathetic. "Don't be afraid," he tells me. "I'll protect you."

Sure enough, he shows up every morning and every evening to escort me, the virgin maiden, to and from work. He is a really fine man, a "mench," as my father would have said. We become friends. I often wish that I could be totally honest with him, but I do not dare expose my real identity. Not yet. Not even as the Russians finally come. Not even now as the defeated Germans disappear into any hiding place they can find, fearing the vengeance of the hostile local population.

One day Pani Bielanska comes back from the marketplace with an annoyed expression on her face. "Guess what I saw at the market?" she exclaims, looking as though she had seen a ghost. "A Jew! Can you believe this? I guess the Germans didn't get rid of all of them after all!"

I could feel my blood curdle, my skin goose-pimple. As my adrenaline takes over I want to do something, to answer her, to run, but for the moment I am paralyzed. It helps to hear Marzena protest, "Well, they have the right to live too!" But for me, the pain and the fear are too deeply ingrained, too deadly to be shrugged off so easily. This from this dear, kind lady, so willing to share her own place with other war refugees!

"Oh Mother, I'm not crazy about Jews either, but God gave them life and only God should take it away from them." Marzena then looks at me, "Why, Basia," she says to me, "why do you have tears in your eyes? Aren't you glad the war is over? Don't cry. We're free now!"

Not really. Not yet! Not free enough to discard my Christian camouflage. Neither free nor safe from the hatred and the anti-Semitism that still pervades this country.

17

News from the Market
Leonia, Spring 1945

Here in Poland, in the tiny town of Rawa Mazowietska, the Russian army has trounced the Germans. They are gone. Church bells are ringing. Families and friends are hugging and embracing. Celebrants waving the Polish flag are singing the long-forbidden national anthem, "Poland Is Still Alive." Young girls decked out in traditional red-and-white Polish costumes, their hair decorated with flowers and ribbons, are parading and dancing in the streets and especially in the market place. The Nazi terror is finally over.

Marzena, her mom, and I are celebrating too. They talk of the life that used to be, and how we all can finally hope to start it again. Marzena still does not know if her husband is dead or alive. She is very concerned about that. She wants to resume her career as a lawyer again, but first she must find out about him. Communications are chaotic. Word of mouth is most important.

When they go back to their city house in Warsaw, they will have a small party for their scattered relatives and friends. They will share both the joys of the final German defeat and the commiserations of what has happened to their Poland. They will exchange information. Perhaps someone will know something about her husband. They are good people and I'm happy for them. My own elation is much more circumspect. The Russian victory is music to my ears too, but who is there left for me to dance with?

I want to take Marzena's hand and say, *Sit down, please. You have been so kind that I want you to know the truth about me. So much of what I have told you is a lie. My real name is not Basia Siudetska, it's Leonia Honigstein Szyfka. I am not a maiden girl from a little farm village. I am a widow, and I have a child in a convent. My husband was killed in the Warsaw Ghetto Uprising. You see, all the sensibilities you have praised me for, assuming that they are the result of my good Catholic upbringing, are Jewish sensibilities. I am a Jew.*

But how can I say this to her in front of her mom, who just yesterday expressed such an aversion to Jews?

So I reveal to her only part of the truth. "You see, "I lie again, "before the war I had a fiancé. He was killed in the Polish army early in the war. We had a baby out of wedlock and she is in a convent now. I must go find her."

There is no need for me to tell her what happened to me yesterday. It was at the market, yes, the very same market where her mother witnessed those undesirable Jewish survivors. But my experience left me with nothing but joy and elation.

There I am, standing near the bakery goods that I am delivering to be sold there, when I see a figure dressed in the familiar all-white habit. I raise my eyes slowly, dubious about the possibility that it might be Sister Bernarda, the one woman who could tell me where my Rachel is at this time. And then our eyes meet. It *is* Sister Bernarda. Slowly a smile lights up her face as it lights up my heart. Her inner beauty still radiates from behind her many new wrinkles. Her arms are spreading out wide as she is reaching out to me.

Even before I ask, she tells me the answer. My Rachel, my Teresa, is okay. It is so good to hear that from the lips of the wonderful woman who has saved so many lives. For a moment nothing else registers for me. In my head there are just two thoughts. "Rachel is alive. The war is over. Rachel is alive."

Then I hear the rest of the story. Rachel and a small group of children and sisters from the original convent are living in Koslo, a little village about sixty kilometers away. Sister is saying that even though the Germans have left, the girls in the convent there are in bad condition. Malnutrition has left many of them in poor health, and their education has been suspended. They are living in substandard housing. The beautiful convent building outside Warsaw is so damaged that they cannot move back into it. But they are alive and the convent will start all over again. There is so much to do. Sister is excited to begin the work.

Then Sister remembers the few pieces of jewelry I gave her when we first met. She wants to know if we can set up a time to meet in Warsaw so she can return them to me. Really I haven't given them a thought in years. The only jewel I want back now is my daughter. I tell Sister to use them to help rebuild the convent she loves. It's all I have to thank her with.

But what happened to Basia, our fairy godmother? Did she survive? Sister shakes her head sadly. "No," she says, "Basia was betrayed by a Jew." Just a few days after she saved Rachel and me, she was walking with a man that she was hoping to save as well. A Nazi officer accosted them to demand their papers. The man did not yet have any. As he was being led away for further questioning, he yelled, "She too is Jewish!" So they were both taken and killed.

There is nothing to be said. Shame at my fellow Jew mingles with sadness about Basia. How strangely war twists our basic ethics. Sister and I both stand in silence and grief.

That same evening I tell Marzena about Rachel. Her face registers only sympathy. She tells me to go and get my child as soon as possible. If I wish to bring her back to her villa, we both are welcome. With her blessing, I set out to find my child.

18

The Road to Koslo
Leonia and Rachel, Spring 1945

Leonia

These forests and farms between Rawa Mazowietska and Koslo have evaded the German bombs. Not much here to attract their attention. There are no significant buildings that might serve their war needs, no major roads to transport slaves or weapons, only small farms with modest cottages and barns and stretches of woods. The locals travel on the same aged dirt and gravel roads where their ancestors have trekked with similar wagons and horses for generations.

Where the spring sun penetrates the bare branches, the snow melts during the day and refreezes at night. In the daytime the slosh drags one's feet; in the evening the icy mud is patchy, uneven, and slippery. Only the winds are untrammeled. They freely push everything in their way. But the most ominous are the other travelers. We eye each other suspiciously. *Are you Polish, or a German enemy that has been abandoned by his army? Are you one of their deserters trudging westward, trying to hide your identity by discarding your uniform? It's too cold to do that unless you steal the clothes from one of our people. We do not trust any of*

you. Now that the twists of war have turned against you, you rightly fear to ask us for food and help.
Bodies of some Germans are swinging from trees, reminding their fellows that they have no friends here. The passersby spit in the direction of the frozen corpses. That expresses the local sentiment. Some strip the dead of their clothing, especially their leather boots.

My own shoes are soaked and my toes are freezing. I spot a dead German soldier lying in the snow with boots still on his feet. The half-frozen face is that of a boy. There are no wrinkles on his smooth skin and just bare frozen peach fuzz on his chin. Just a German teenager, an innocent peg in the Nazi war game, just fodder for the Russian army. I register all that and I'm surprised that no sympathy wells up in me. I feel nothing at all as I peel off his boots. My only regret is that they do not fit better. They are too big, of two different sizes, and both are for the left foot. Perhaps he had peeled them off other bodies. No matter. They are better than mine. I stuff them with socks and walk on.

The farmers in the area are unsophisticated people, religious and usually kind. They have little education. They tend to be very respectful and deferential to anyone that comes from a big city like Warsaw. It is their tradition to be generous to travelers. Whatever fare they have, they share, be it a bit of straw on the floor of their hut or even in the barn. I'm grateful to be allowed to spend the nights with them and eat whatever they are generous enough to share.

The woman who answers the door on my second night of walking recognizes my Warsaw accent and is impressed in spite of the fact that I am filthy and wearing just a bunch of rags. She asks her husband to bring fresh straw into the hut for me, "the lady from Warsaw." After a long, cold day of walking, I know I will sleep well anywhere I can lie down, especially after they are kind enough to divide up with me their potato and cabbage soup. It's warm and appetizing and I believe I even taste some ham. What a treat!

Dusk comes on quickly. Just as my hosts are about to extinguish the candles so we can all sleep, the farmer's wife suddenly shouts out that the "lady"—that's me—should not have to sleep like a peasant in the straw. The lady should share the marital bed, the only real bed in the house, with herself.

"Hey," she yells to her husband, "Are you going to let this lady from Warsaw sleep in the hay while a yokel like you lies here with me?" Poor guy. I know he does not want to give up his warm place in the bed, but he reluctantly acquiesces to his wife's wish. Clearly she is the boss here. I too am almost asleep and quite content where I am, but my protests are also completely ignored. I am forced to trade places with the husband and get in bed with his wife. I'm barely asleep again when something pricks my neck. Rubbing does not help. The pricking is getting worse. Rest does not come as I had expected. It's lice. They smell fresh new blood and attack me everywhere. I twitch and scratch and shift. There must be hundreds of them. It's a losing battle. I'm tossing and turning. Neither the wife nor I can sleep.

"What is the matter?" she queries. "Aren't you comfortable?"

I'm stymied. I try to cover all exposed parts of me with my clothes. They are no obstacles to the bugs. It's no use. How can I tell this good woman that the fleas and lice that no longer bother her are feasting on every part of my body? If there's any part of me left by sunrise I will be glad to get on the road again.

"Oh, I'm just very nervous because it's a long trip. I have to leave very early tomorrow but I am very thankful for your kind hospitality," I answer her.

Four days later I reach Koslo. It's a very small town. I have no trouble at all finding out where the children from the convent Niepokalanek are living. The very first farmer I ask tells me it's just down the road, the first structure after the next left turn. He assures me I will have no trouble finding it, even though it has no markers. He hesitates a moment and obviously wants to be helpful, but can't seem to think of anything. "I wish I had something to give you for the sisters, but nothing is growing yet."

Sure enough I soon see a single-story building that from the outside looks more like a barn than anything else. I enter it somewhat apprehensively. It has been two years since I've seen Rachel. I've heard stories about children who have bonded with their caretakers, who do not recognize their parents, and who refuse to go with them.

I am dismayed at the primitive conditions inside. Straw mattresses covered with blankets line the walls. A few bare wooden tables and benches are the only other furnishings. Of course the move was forced by the Nazis and done in haste, but even so, these are miserable accommodations.

The sisters accept my identity without any question, even though none of them have ever met me before. They point to one of the smaller children sitting on her heels on a makeshift mattress. Yes, there she is, that's Teresa, as though I could not pick out my own child, my

Rachel. I get goose bumps all over my body, and do a silent prayer of gratitude. I thank God for this moment when my own daughter and I are in the same room at last. We have survived the war. I have found her. Gratitude wells up within me. In silence I know that only a very few are as lucky as I am.

The sisters call the children to stand up and to welcome me. They do not identify me other than as Pani Siudetska. Like all the others, Rachel stands up, murmurs the proper greeting, and sits down. There was not a glimmer of recognition in her eyes. She and another girl go back to whatever they were doing—something with a paper and pencil. She is taller, thinner, with some baby teeth missing. She is scratching her head, messing up the small braids behind each ear. I wonder if she too has lice, like the farmers that I met along the way. I do not approach her or make any moves toward her. I must be cautious and not scare her. The sisters understand. They say I can stay here a few days to regain Rachel/Teresa's confidence. They put out a mattress for me among themselves. I wish I could repay these kind sisters for all their care.

The next day I see the situation more clearly. The children are thin with large stomachs. They seem fragile, lethargic. Most of them, including my Rachel, are quite skinny and they have bowed legs. The sisters tell me that most of them have bleeding gums. There are no dentists available. Yes, they have lice in their hair. They have insufficient clothing and their shoes are just sandals that provide no protection in the snow. The sisters are overwhelmed with their burdens and too genteel to take aggressive action in order to improve their situation.

What an outrage! How can it be that even now, with the war over, these orphans are still cold and starved, while *volksdeutsch* families in the area are most probably well equipped with stocks of fine provisions? Why is it that no one is doing anything about this? I request a basket and the addresses of some of the German families.

The first German family I confront is occupying one of the very nicest of the local homes. The hausfrau is plump, warm, dressed in a heavy wool sweater that fits over her ample hips. Behind her is her husband, husky and stern. He appears to be in great shape, and I'll bet he has a gun somewhere nearby. They protest that they have no hidden food stock. Really! They offer me potatoes, but "That is all we have," they insist. My stomach tightens with anger, but I leave because I am afraid. I do not want to wind up dead in their cellar.

On the way to the next home I pass some local youths pelting each other with snowballs. They are having a rowdy fight and clearly they enjoy it. These are farm kids, used to plenty of hard work, and their muscles show it. Their language is coarse. They are not squeamish about a bit of rough stuff either.

"Hey boys," I call out to them, "I need some help to get some food from the Germans and to help the orphans at the convent. Any of you willing to help?" And how!! They all jump at the prospect. "Only two of you, please!" They argue among themselves for a minute and soon I have two strong young bulls escorting me to the next German home. I feel much more secure with them at my side.

Our new target owners are initially just as unyielding, but they are eyeing the youths guardedly. I suggest that the boys would like to inspect their home. Perhaps they have some food they have forgotten about.

Suddenly there is a change in their attitude. They will be happy to donate some of their provisions for the benefit of the poor orphans in the convent. They had no idea there was such a shortage of food there. No idea at all. They bring out a bit of butter and sugar and jam. We demand more. We get eggs and some dried apples. Now more experienced, we visit another *volksdeutsch* family with good results. They are able to spare just a bit of flour. Oh! And because they feel so sad for the poor orphans they will even give us their last bit of dried plums. We visit a few more families. In triumph the boys and I return to the convent with bread, eggs, butter, sugar, and luxury items they haven't seen in years. They are amazed and grateful. We invite the boys to come feast with us, even though they look like they have bottomless appetites, making us silently grateful when they decline. There will be more for the sisters and the girls.

Now my mind is not so much on the food as on Rachel. In the two years that we haven't seen each other she has become more serious looking. When I take some steps in her direction she seems to be shrinking away from me. She is definitely mine, but I don't think she remembers me at all. How am I going to approach her? How can I hug her without frightening her? She seems so fragile, so quiet, so distant. Where is the happy dancing effervescent child that was mine before this war? Will I be able to find the means to give her back the health, the energy, the confidence that used to be there? How do I regain her trust, how do I replace that lost joy in her life? I know that her safety zone, all that is familiar to her, is here in the convent. The idea of leaving this place with me, a stranger to her, might frighten her. I must restrain myself and allow some time to get reacquainted with my own daughter. But I don't have time. We must go soon. And I can't even tell her where we will be living, or how we will manage.

Rachel

For three days I am aware that this lady is watching me. Even my friend Luba notices it. When she and I are playing cards, the lady walks over to us. She watches us for a short while and smiles. But when she has left, Luba says, "I think that lady, Pani Siudetska, was smiling at you. Do you know her?"

I don't know anybody like that. All I know is that she is the lady who brought us some good food, and that she has been watching me. Could she be interested in taking me away from here? We all know that the war is over, and the sisters have told us that some of our relatives might be coming back to get us. So far only a very few mothers have come back for their children.

There is nothing about her that is familiar to me. Not her face, not her manner, not her way of talking. I have not even had a picture of my mother during all the time I have been here. There have been no letters or messages between us. I can't recall her face. I don't remember her at all. Actually I hardly even think about her anymore. Until now that is. I try to remember what she looked like, and there is nothing there. Nothing.

Perhaps this lady is looking for her daughter, and she thinks it might be me but she isn't sure. I just don't know. If she decides to take me, then that will prove that I am her daughter, or that she thinks that I am. I don't know if that is what I want or not. I think I will be worried if she picks me and disappointed if she doesn't. What am I going to do if she picks me and then doesn't like me?

At last Sister Ena calls for me. "The lady who has been with us these last few days is really your mother. It's been a long time since you were with her. Maybe you don't remember her, but she came a long way to get you because she loves you very much. She will take you away from us but you will always be in our hearts too. You are a very lucky girl! Go spend some time with her now. You will be going together tomorrow morning, so say good-bye to all your friends tonight." She beams me a smile full of confidence and happiness at my good fortune. I am not excited. I don't have any idea of what I feel. Now that it's happened, I don't know how to feel.

When I walk over to "my mother," she starts to put her arms around me. I can sense she is somewhat hesitant about it. I am too. I try to hug her back just as Sister suggested. She holds me close for a moment. I'm not sure I like the feeling. It's very unnatural. I can't remember when I was hugged last. My mother? Should I call her "ma'am," or "Mom?" I want to examine everything about her face and to ask her a thousand questions, but I don't even know what questions. How do I start? I want her to think that I am competent and that I am smart and efficient so that I will not be too much of a burden. I concentrate on doing the right thing, like showing her my clothes and folding them carefully so we can pack them. There is an extra pair of underwear, another blouse, my sweater, a hat, and a jacket.

"Well, we won't have to carry much, since you will need to wear almost everything here. You can even put on the extra underpants to help keep you warm."

I'm shocked a little by her casual reference to "underpants." It's kind of a no-no to mention anything like that. But she seems nice. I'm still scared. I try to act happy.

Saying good-bye is not too hard. I'm comfortable with the sisters and the other girls here but I don't have any special friends. Even Luba is not particularly distressed that I'm leaving. All the sisters pat me on the shoulder and say, "Don't forget us," or "Don't forget to go to church on Sunday." They all bless me and wish both my new mom and me a good trip. I know they mean it and I'm sad to leave them. They have been my guardian angels for a long time.

My new mom and I leave together the next morning. She is carrying a small bundle of our clothes. I'm wearing almost everything I own. It's very cold. My mother holds my hand. That is a very nice feeling. I'm not used to being held like that. I'm not used to being held at all. I do not ask anything. I must get used to calling this lady my mom. No one told me where we would be going, only that now that the war is over, Mom and I must start a new life together.

Rochelle Dreeben

19

With Strangers
Rachel, Late Spring 1945

The reason that Mom leaves me here at this farmhouse every day is because after we started this journey together, I just couldn't walk anymore. We had already walked a very long time and the day was getting darker. It was so cold, and getting colder. The mushy, half-frozen snow was bumpy and slippery. My sandals were stiff, and my feet hurt so much in them that I just begged her to let me lie down right there. I didn't care what happened to me. But she cajoled me and pulled me and sometimes almost carried me until we saw this farmhouse. All I wanted was someplace warm. I couldn't even feel my legs, but she made me push on one step at a time and we both prayed the owners of this house would let us in. Mom was worried too. She told me that kindness to strangers is traditional here, but with the war just ended, people are afraid.

We were so lucky. These good people not only let us in and immediately told us to sit by the fire; they gave us some hot soup too. They didn't even ask us any questions until after we thawed out a little. When Mom explained to them that we had just been reunited at the convent, and that she needed to get me back to our home (I wondered what home she was talking about), they were so sympathetic, and completely understanding. They even said we could stay here a few days, and Mom could help the farmer's wife with the bread making so as to earn some money. They are so nice I wish they were our real family. So here we are. I dread having to go walking in the cold again.

It has been five days of luxury for me, especially when I get to sit on the rocking chair. The first time I did, I asked Pani Gosia if I might do so when there is no one home. She laughed and assured me, "Of course you may." When I do sit there, and rock in front of the fire, I do feel somewhat guilty because both she and my mom are working so hard. But I only sit there when they are away.

With the first light of the dawn, while I'm still half asleep, I smell yeast rising. They have already been working a long time. With my eyelids still closed, I feel the day slowly growing brighter. I can hear the crackling of the fire and feel the blessed heat from the oven coming to me in waves from the other side of the room. Pani Gosia is telling my mother where she will need to go today to sell the bread they have baked. Also what my mother will need to bring back from the market for tomorrow's baking.

As soon as the bread is done and has cooled off just a little, my mother puts it all in a big sack to carry it to the local markets. I don't know where she is going because I have not been outside this farm. She will not be back until almost dusk. Then she will return loaded down with sacks filled with flour. I think it must be a pretty long trip. I know the bread is very heavy from the way she is bent over when she lifts the sack onto her back and the way she leans over when she walks.

Whenever she returns it's late in the day and her face is red from the cold. I rush to help her unload. She straightens out slowly and takes a big breath, then walks over to the fire to rub her hands together. Her fingers are marked with red welts and bruises from the ropes she held to keep the sacks on her back. Even the heavy cloth wrapped around the ropes doesn't fully protect her hands. She is so tired she can't even eat or talk until she has some rest. Both the farmer and his wife are tired too. They have been working all day getting their land ready for planting. I have put out the dishes and some salt and pepper on the table. I can hardly wait for supper. It's my big event of the day. It always consists of wonderful soup and that homemade bread and white farmer's cheese. There is almost no conversation. We all go to bed almost as soon as we finish eating. Mom and I don't talk much ever. I know she is too tired and I don't want to ask too many questions.

It's good here. I enjoy each day without any plans for tomorrow. I watch the rooster chase the chickens around in the yard, and I check for any eggs that have been laid. I peel the potatoes for our supper. I sweep the floor. I help the farmer's wife carry some of the animal feed or clean straw for the cow in the barn, but the farmer's wife does not want me to carry the milk because she is afraid I might spill it. It is her bartering staple.

The fresh milk is precious. Neighboring farmers bring pork or other food to trade for milk or cream. Some want the cheese that she makes daily. She skims the cream from the milk and puts it into a very clean piece of cotton cloth, then ties it securely and hangs it over a big pot. It drips and drips for several days until most of the liquid goes down into the pot and the cheese is almost solid. I think that is why it is called "farmer's cheese." We never had any in the convent. It's very delicious. Nothing goes to waste. We drink the liquid in the pot just as it is. Other times it is used for cooking.

Mom and I sleep very close to where the cheese is dripping. She falls asleep almost instantly after we blow out the candles. The cheese continues to plop, plop, plop all through the night. Mom snores. I try to keep track of how many cheese plops there are to every one of Mom's snores. Sometimes there are two plops. Sometimes there are three. They are not always even. I lose count pretty fast and I can't remember anyway.

The farmers have been very kind and Mom thanks them again and again. They thank Mom, too, for all the help with the bread. They have arranged for a neighbor who is going to the city of Lodz to take us there in his horse and buggy. So we are leaving today. I know he is getting paid, and some of his payment is in the bread, which is also traveling with us to the big city. We bury ourselves in the piles of fresh straw in the back of the buggy and enjoy its smell and that of the warm bread. It's still cold outside. I don't have any real shoes yet. I am so happy not to have to walk! While we are enjoying our ride I learn a little bit about the place where we are going.

Mom asks the driver to take us to a specific address. He tells us that he knows the area. It is near the market where he is going, so it's not much out of the way. He delivers us onto a street lined with two-story, red brick houses. Each looks like a palace to me. Except for some taped window cracks here and there, most of the houses are in good condition. Mom knows a woman who owns one of them, and we can stay there for a few days. She learned about her from Sister Bernarda when they met in the market. Sister Bernarda helped save a lot of people, and this lady was one of them.

The lady who answers the bell, standing at her front door to greet us, does not look like most of the women I see. Her hair is arranged with lots of locks high on her head. And she does not wear a scarf that covers them up either. I like the pretty white buttons on her pleated navy dress, which is partly covered by a heavy sweater. Her shoes are pretty too. They are very shiny, and they even have a high heel. Mom tells me her lips are so red because she is wearing lipstick. Her skin is rather pale. That is just the opposite of how my mother and most of the ladies look. Their cheeks are ruddy, probably from the farm work and the cold. Their lips are just plain like my own. I'm not sure I like this lipstick, and I wonder where does she get all these fancy things? Then she smiles to greet us and I notice one of her teeth is missing. That is common enough.

She gives my mom a big warm hug, and then she squeezes my shoulders and tells me to call her Pani Lubia. I like her smile and I'm glad she didn't try to hug or kiss me. I smile too. She invites us in for some soup and we also share the bread that my mother brought. What a great day. First riding in the hay, and seeing a big city, and now a good meal.

Pani Lubia's house has a couple of rooms plus a big kitchen with a big wood floor. There is almost no furniture except for a metal table and some odd chairs. Pani Lubia tells us that almost everything else was stolen or sold. She is grateful to be able to have this house that her family owned before the war. Both she and my mom talk about how courageous and wonderful Sister Bernarda is. She had arranged jobs for Pani Lubia just like she did for my mom. Mom tells me that the man who is living here with her is not her husband, just a very good friend. Her husband was probably killed, as was the rest of her family. None have come back. She has already been to Warsaw to see if any of her relatives were listed among the registered survivors, but found none. I know from the conversations I overhear that Mom also plans to go to Warsaw to check out that register. I secretly hope that she might find my father, but I'm afraid to mention it. I think it bothers her when I ask such questions.

Mom leaves for Warsaw the very next day. Pani Lubia is wonderful to me. She still calls me Teresa and whispers to me that we must continue to pretend to be Catholic and to wear the crosses around our necks. It's safer that way. Of course I want to wear my cross. It's been my special protection for a long time. I don't see why I should have to pretend anything. After all, I really am a Catholic. Or perhaps I am still a Jew. It's confusing.

Pani Lubia takes me to the town square and we enter a shoemaker's store. It has a huge pair of boots hanging next to a sign in front of it. I'm going to get a pair of real leather shoes. The man from the store and Pani Lubia are both taking great care that the measurements of my foot will provide plenty of room for some extra thick socks and for future growth. They will have laces that go all the way up to my ankles. The shoemaker will make them just for me in a few days. I don't even dare show how excited that makes me. It's important to control my feelings. I know that my mother earned the money for them when she was hauling the bread and flour on her back.

At the market Pani Lubia tells me that there is not much variety of vegetables as yet because it's only spring and the new crops are not out. She buys some potatoes and cabbage and meat bones. Meat bones, that is really special. I wonder if we are going to get to suck on them. In any case they will make that soup really good. My tongue is already anticipating this meal.

She points to an empty building that has been badly damaged. "That was the synagogue," she says as though I should know what a synagogue is. Whatever it is, it's mostly ruined. There is a cemetery next to it with a lot of broken stones, and it's a mess, as well. A lot of places look like that. We also pass a church and I know Sunday will be soon. I do need to go to church, like we always did at the convent, but I don't know how to ask to go. I have some concerns about my loyalty. I don't think that my mother or Pani Lubia will be going.

When we get back, Pani Lubia tells me it's time for my bath. She fills up a special large basin with water that she warmed on the stove and sets it on the table in the kitchen. "Take off your clothes and get in the tub," she tells me, as though it was a perfectly normal thing to do. But her friend is there. I'm almost eight years old! Does she really expect me to strip in front of a man? "Why aren't you getting in the tub?" she asks. "Come here, I'll help you!"

Her hands remove my blouse and skirt and then she just pulls down my underpants. I'm standing there completely naked in front of these people! In front of a man! She washes my whole body and even my hair while they converse in a most casual manner. I'm so terribly ashamed, but I don't know what to do. What would the sisters say if they knew? They always stressed modesty even with no men around. There, when I had to wash, I tried to not even look at my own body. My face is burning. I can't face either one of them. Pani Lubia and her friend are just talking about what they saw at the market. They act as though nothing unusual is happening.

Afterwards Pani Lubia hands me some clean clothes. I don't know where she got them. They smell so fresh. They feel wonderful on my skin and I thank her for them, but I still can't look her in the face. That night as I lie on my cot I wonder how I can feel so good even though I am so disgraced. When my mother returns should I tell her about this? Will she understand? If we are still here, what shall I do about going to church on Sunday?

20

One Plus One
Leonia, Spring 1945

Warsaw is changing once again. There are signs of revival among the ruins. Workers are sorting out the remains of the bombed buildings. Anything made of wood has disappeared long ago, probably used for heating purposes. Heaps of pipes and metal are being separated from piles of cement and stones. They will all be resurrected into new structures. There are piles of just bricks too. Even a brick needs the company of its own kind to become a significant entity.

The city where I spent the first thirty years of my life is gone. Not just the stores and apartment houses where the current fashions once decorated the windows, not just the smells of bakeries and butcher shops and elegant cafés, not just the ghetto now lying in ashes, but the faces, the friendly familiar faces that used to smile at me. Somewhere, someone I care about must still be alive! There were so many of us before the war. Surely some have survived; maybe a member of my family or even just a friend. I don't dare to hope, but I do.

That is why I left my daughter, Rachel, with my friend Lubia. I have heard that Jewish survivors are registering in a little room in a building on Tlomacki Place. A small, handwritten sign near the door identifies it as the Jewish Historical Institute. The corner building next to it was once a synagogue. One half is still standing erect while the other half has been sheared off about halfway down. As I look up I see pigeons fighting for the remaining space under the eaves. They too must relocate.

I walk up the stairs slowly, aware of the echo of each footstep bouncing off the bare walls of this empty building. The room, located on the second floor, is as bare of Jewish memorabilia as the country itself is stripped of my people. No one is waiting.

A young woman sits at a small table staring into space. Neither her appearance nor her manner inspires my confidence in the seriousness of this endeavor. There is a pencil and a notebook on the table. It's the type of notebook distributed to second graders to practice their letters. Those who have the courage to do so write down their own names and hope that some family member or friend will contact them.

I search through the names already there. Some, like Kristofer Alenki, are obviously not even Jewish names. I glance at the woman behind the table and notice that she is wearing a cross. Is she Jewish? She understands my puzzlement. "As you know, many of our people are still afraid to publicly declare their real identity. I caution people that they cannot be found without their real names, but some refuse to take a chance. They think this might be another trick to entrap them."

I understand their fear. Anti-Semitism is still rampant. We are no longer in danger from the Germans, but we are in great peril from the Polish populace, especially from those who took over Jewish property and are determined to keep it.

Even though the names are not alphabetized, it does not take me long to check out the few pages. There are fewer than a hundred names. The remainder of the Jewish populace that once comprised a third of the city and ten percent of the country now fits into just a few pages of that notebook. None of them is familiar.

When I return a few days later however, I do find a familiar name. Moses Schleifstein. A friend of my youth—more than a friend, a relative in a way. Before the war his sister Hela married my eldest brother Heniek, so he also became a part of our family.

I doubt that Hela or Heniek or their children, Mory and Gutka, are alive. Probably Moses lost his wife, and his daughter too. We were all friends, and our daughters played together. His daughter and Rachel were just six months apart. But that was all long, long ago. The last

Moses Schleifstein at age 20

time I saw Moses was early in the war, at the bar mitzvah of our nephew Mory, before the full enormity of the tragedy that was coming was evident to us. He had come alone then, afraid to bring his wife and daughter. I can't wait to see him now. Maybe, just maybe, there is someone else still living. The address he wrote down is not far. I am hurrying there right now.

Walking away from Tlomacki Place, I walk toward Market Street, the commercial center of the city. Today it is just a passageway between heaps of wreckage and an occasional still-standing building.

All at once I feel rather than see eyes that are piercing me, eyes riveted on me. With some concern I look toward the other side of the street from whence the look comes. A young, thin man is there, staring directly at me. He is wearing a cap that shades his face and he holds his hand over his eyes to shield them from the brilliant afternoon sun. I cannot see his face but there is something familiar about his figure and the way he stands. I stop walking and shade my own eyes as well. I squint. My heart jumps. My head is saying, "Slow down, it's just a mirage." Could I be hallucinating? Blood drains from my face. I gasp and reach out to a pile of wood to support myself. Could it be Adam, the youngest of my six brothers?

We eye each other furtively, afraid of being mistaken. Do I dare hope? Can I risk the disappointment? A small crowd of people surrounds me to ask what the problem is. My tongue doesn't work. My body isn't responding. I am paralyzed, unable to answer, unable to cross the street.

I watch as the figure across the street moves toward me. I cannot see the face because the cap on his head still shades his face. But his height and his gait continue to be familiar to me. Why is his pace so slow? Can't he see I can't move? Almost as though he could read my thought he removes the cap. I can see him well now. I gasp. I'm almost positive that the face is that of my youngest brother, Adam.

The people, the noise, the street all recede. There is only this apparition moving from across the street. Yes! Definitely! Adam! Finally he is within two feet of me. The too-large jacket he is wearing and the baggy pants make his frame look even smaller than I remember, but it is he. Moments of quiet pass while we examine each other with our eyes, each of us wondering what to say, what to ask first. I see him open his mouth and hesitate. I understand what he wants to know.

"Rachel is alive too," I say. He closes his eyes as though his prayer has been granted. Now we can hug. Now there are at least two of us, and Rachel makes three. He tells me about his girlfriend Meriam. I tell him about Moses. That makes five of us. There are those I can talk to and trust. We are a family now.

21

Photographs
Leonia, Late Spring 1945

We are all in Warsaw now, our family of five, living in this room that is like a cave among the ruins. We just climb up over the piles of cement and broken bricks as though they were terraces, up to what must have been a second-floor apartment. A former window is now our

Meriam Waisman Honigstein and
Moses Schleifstein in Warsaw, 1945

front door. We don't worry about any company. Our two
rooms here are our haven and our shelter. Adam and
Meriam, always enterprising, had laid claim to this place
as soon as they found it. Finders keepers, for now at least,
while records are unobtainable. It is in an excellent loca-
tion, close to the heart of what used to be the main shopping area, Warsaw's Market Street.

The rooms are small but big enough to hold all our
furniture and things. This includes a bed in one room,
and the wardrobe turned into a second bed in the other.
It is just as hard as the floor, but it feels better, warmer.
Moses had moved in with us too, just soon as we found
each other. Sometimes Rachel sleeps with Adam and
Meriam, other times with Moses and me. With three of us
in one small bed, and our coats for extra covers, we are
pretty warm. But sleep is difficult for me now.

All through the war I kept four photographs in a
special pouch that fit right next to my body inside my
undergarments. They are the little puzzle pieces of my
past, a past that was not completely destroyed as long as I
had those. Of course during the war I had to keep them
all hidden, a forbidden secret, so that no one should
chance upon them and ask, "Who is that little girl?"

They are all pictures of Rachel. Finely crafted, pro-
fessional studio photographs in sepia, mounted like
postcards on fine paper, with borders and serrated edges.
There is one for each of the first four years of her life,
each carefully posed, a photographic work of art. I remember how carefully I chose them from among the
many we had accumulated. Two years is a long time to
remember. Even a mother's memory fades.

During moments of dreadful sadness and loneli-
ness, when I was sure that no one would interrupt my

distraction, I would take out my treasures. There she is, three years old, dressed in the white organza outfit that my brother Heniek had sent from Paris before the war. She is leaning over a rose bush, delicately smelling its fragrance. Her lacy underpants are sticking out beneath the dress. And there she is in another photograph, even younger, with her short curly locks framing her face, delighted with herself and her own first steps, her face aglow with success. And there she is in a tutu, her hand up in the air, dancing, dancing. I remembered the happiness of those moments, and how they renewed my resolve to persevere through the war and to see her again.

None of those pictures are of my husband, Joshua, because his Semitic looks could endanger my life. He was most insistent about that even though he knew that if Rachel and I survived, she would never know her father's face. There are none of my own parents either, or other members of our family, for the same reason. And how many pictures can one fit under one's garments without a suspicious bulk showing through?

I treasure those pictures. Even now that the war is finally over and it is legal for us to exist, these pictures are my most valued possession. Rachel loves to look at them too. She cannot recognize herself and asks many times, "Is that really me?" Sometimes I think she fears that if that little girl does not look like herself, then I might not be her real mother.

We still continue to pass ourselves off as gentiles even though we are no longer in mortal fear of the German Gestapo. Normal rules of society are slowly, slowly reasserting themselves. I have taken my precious photographs and put them into a special wallet that I keep in my purse. There is seldom any money in it so I rarely need to take it out to pay for something. I never leave it in our room, which cannot be properly locked. There is still too much greed and thievery in this society.

I am in the bakery opening my purse to pay for my purchase. Immediately I sense that something is awry. Something is amiss. It's my wallet. My photographs are missing! I can't believe this. There was no cash there, and I always hold my purse tight, right under my arm. How could anyone take anything out of it without my knowledge? I search my purse again and again. No wallet! No pictures!

That small collection of my past has been stolen. The thief will surely just throw my treasures into the trash. A flood of grief that I have held in all those years overcomes me. I run out of the bakery. Everything about my past is trash, just trash.

When Moses comes in I tell him about it and he tries to comfort me. We will go to a photographer as soon as we can and we will all have fine pictures made, he promises. Rachel is still young, he tells me. We will still have some pictures of her childhood. But we both know that they will not replace those that were stolen. So many of those I love are gone, and now even these paper memories have been taken away.

When Rachel comes home and I am still crying she is alarmed. She has never seen me cry like this before. I have been stoic all through the war and now I am losing control over pictures. Just silly pictures, I tell myself! But what will I say the next time she asks to see them again?

I force myself to calm down. "Our photographs are gone, they were stolen from me," I say as calmly as I can. I must be positive. I don't want her to know how badly this affects me.

22

Night Demons
Rachel, Fall 1946

I don't know how long we have been living here in these ruins, but now I hate it. I didn't at first. It's not that I mind our surroundings. They don't matter at all. It's just that I'm afraid all the time. I can't eat or sleep or stop thinking about it. I just cannot get that corpse out of my mind.

Everybody is trying to help me. Yesterday Meriam decided to make me an "egg-rosette." She took two eggs, as precious as they are, and beat them very hard with a fork and then put them in our new frying pan, which Uncle Adam got from somewhere in the market. Then she put the pan on our new burner, and as the eggs hardened she pushed a small area of the mix from the outside to the center of the pan. Each push created shapes that looked like the petals of a rose. She told me her mom used to make them for her just like that. Those were the most beautiful eggs I ever saw. At first I hesitated to eat them because they were so pretty. Then I gobbled them up. They were delicious too. Especially because I was really hungry

When Mom comes back to our home she brings some of that plain white stuff that I really like. Usually I can't wait for her to start cutting it up into small squares.

They are called "skwarki" after they are fried and crisp like Mom makes them. They are so delicious that I just want them right away, even though they are still raw. I sneak one off the board when she isn't looking and try it. It is soft and slippery and mild and it just glides into my mouth then slides down my throat. They are so good that I must have more, so I keep sneaking them. Mom must have seen me. She is looking at me like I'm strange. "You like these?" I assure her I love them, but what are they? "Well, they're bacon fat. I was planning to fry these, but now they are almost all gone." Mom is not mad at me at all. She seems glad that I ate them. Maybe it's because yesterday I refused to eat anything at all.

Then Moses goes out to the market and comes back with a live chicken. Everybody is so excited. They all help to kill it, to de-feather it and to cook it. Moses keeps saying what a great feast it will be. He has not had a chicken in a very long time. They really look forward to this meal. At dinner they all say that it is the best chicken they ever tasted. Adam picked out the breastbone and said that when he and Mom were children, they and their five brothers all fought for it. There was always a mad scramble and a lot of yelling and then whoever got it could make a wish, and then break the bone, and that wish would come true. Then he takes it out and offers it to me. How repulsive!

But to me it is just a dead corpse. It is disgusting. It makes me nauseous. I had seen them preparing it, and I knew right away that I would never eat it. Its pale dead skin is revolting. It reminds me of that ghastly dead body that followed me down Market Street the day I was going to meet Uncle Adam. The one that is still so much with me, even though it was already a week ago. It just will not leave me alone.

"Now really, Rachel, it's not the dead thing that will harm you, you only have to worry about the living ones." That's what they all tell me.

But their words are just words. They do not make me feel any better. All I am aware of right now is that the hair on my arms is standing up, my stomach feels queasy, my heart is beating, and the taste in my throat is awful. It is all because of that hideous decaying body that was carried on a canvas stretcher just a few feet behind me. I know it wanted to swallow me. It was a horrible corpse, not at all like a normal dead person. Those I had seen before, and though they all looked dreadful and sad, they had no power. This one had vibes that aimed straight at me. This one meant to seize me and make me just like its own half-decomposed, sickening self.

It had been dug up somewhere among the ruins of this bombed-out city. There was no cover over it. Two men were carrying it to a more appropriate burial place. The ghastly color of the skin, the purple blotches, the dirty claws at the end of the black fingers that hung over the stretcher paralyzed me. One dull eye, still open, was staring at me with deadly intent. Each ghoulish part etched itself into my mind as I ran to escape. I couldn't run fast enough because there was just a small cleared pathway between the rubble. I couldn't get away. It kept right behind me. Even its putrid stench, embedded in the breeze, pursued my every step.

I ran as fast as I could. As fast as the narrow passageway chiseled between the graves of the ruins and the people crowding the path allowed. As fast as I could without colliding with the merchants who had set up their wares along the sides. This was Market Street, or at least it had been before the war. Mom had sent me here with a message for my uncle, who was looking for something to buy or to sell. I needed to run fast, faster, before the corpse could overtake me, before the smell suffocated me. Before I threw up all my insides.

Did I faint? Did I trip on the debris? Did I just lose consciousness? I don't know.

When I regained awareness, I was back in our home. I was lying on the wardrobe turned into a bed. Mom said, "Thank God Adam was just coming toward you when you fell down. He carried you home. Whatever happened?"

My Uncle Adam and my mother were both puzzled since I did not appear hurt. No hoodlums had attacked me. No anti-Semitic curses had been spit at me. I had no physical injuries.

Since that day I cannot shake the curse of that corpse. It's always there. It is not dead. It comes to life each night and seeks me out.

I usually awake shaking when it's just about to pounce on me. My heart thumps rapid-fire. I'm too scared to sleep. I'm too scared to throw it off. I don't want to call out and upset everybody. Half awake, I try to rationalize; it's just a dream, right? Right, but it's here, just as real, just at the edge of my consciousness, and I know it will recur the second I try to sleep again. I know this nightmare is going to follow me everywhere for the rest of my life! I'm scared, terrified at a future of endless nights with this demon always with me.

This evening I eat only the cabbage soup and the potato. Really it's enough. I don't want to even see the chicken they are all enjoying so much. Poor chicken. Poor me.

23

Amber from Gdansk
Rachel, Late Winter 1946

Mom and Moses are married now. At least that is what I think, even though I never saw any ceremony. Mom has asked me to call him Dad. I like him well enough, but it makes me very uncomfortable to call him "Dad." It makes me feel disloyal to my own dad and to his memory. I avoid addressing Moses as much as possible. He has a job with the government of Poland and we have had to move to a place called Gdansk. I don't know what he does but I think he is some sort of director of a factory. I don't even know what they make. I don't ask either. Instead I keep my ears open and learn a lot that way.

Hushed tones waft toward me from the next room. I hear my mother's soft voice and the lower tones of Moses. Their soft voices penetrate the walls of our newly acquired, elegant home in Gdansk. Though it sits solid and detached, armored with red brick and surrounded by a heavy blanket of virgin snow, I can tell from their voices that they are worried.

They are whispering of rumors that do not bode well. I hear Moses say that the blood-red Marxist star is extending an ever-firmer grip on Poland. That there are rumors of massacres of Jews in a town called Kielce. We are all wary as the late-afternoon crimson rays settle over the pristine white expanse outside.

Even though I'm absorbed in making my miniature doll carriages, the tone of their voices makes me listen intently. I sense their apprehension. It infects me as well.

"You know, Leonia, I have just been made the director of the factory."

"Director? What happened to Mr. Slonski?"

"That's what I asked."

"And?"

"No one would tell me, like he never existed."

"What about Jerzy?"

"He took me aside and told me about the massacre at Kielce. Then he advised me to keep my mouth shut, ask no questions, and do whatever they wanted."

It's less than two months since we were transferred here from Warsaw. Moses has been given a pretty good position by the communist government. The transfer seemed like a very good move. It got us out of a bad living situation in Warsaw, where we had also gotten a nice two-room apartment from the government. Above us lived a young Pole who was habitually drunk. He was always at our door needing something or just looking for someone to have a drink with. Mom was especially anxious when Moses was away. Even after the drunk fell down the stairs and broke both his arms, he still seemed dangerous. But here in Gdansk we are assigned a single house, all to ourselves. We feel safer without anyone so close to us.

This house has been well maintained by its previous occupants. Almost certainly they were some German family that couldn't flee fast enough when the Russians came. They left all this handsome furniture, oriental rugs,

Leonia, Rachel, and Moses in Gdansk,
Poland, 1945

even some fine china. Mom speculates about where each
of these fine items came from. The red Oriental rug in the
main room could well have come from my mother's
family. She even knows the name of the pattern, Baktiary.
The china may have belonged to some Polish aristocrat or
maybe a well-off Jewish merchant. My mother said that
during the war when she was working as a housemaid to
a *volksdeutsch* family, they too had the best of everything

I'm learning a lot about this city, and about what is
happening politically, from the conversations at our
supper table. Gdansk is an important port on the Baltic
Sea. No ruins here. The Germans never bombed it because during the war, it was mostly their own people
occupying it. Over the decades it has changed hands
many times between Germany and Poland. The Germans
call it Danzig. The Polish call it Gdansk.

Now that Russia has liberated Poland, her young
soldiers, still wild with victory, roam the streets in
drunken abandon. In pairs and trios they support each
other while looking for girls and more vodka. Their
strong young voices bellow out *"Moskwa Maya"* (My

137

Moscow) and "*Na Pozytzyi Dzievuszka*" (My Country Girl),
songs of longing for their own towns in Mother Russia
and for their friends back home. Some of them lack an
arm. Some lack an eye. Their cheeks are ruddy from a
tough winter. Their uniforms are worn and patched. Most
of the leather of their boots is gone. But they are victori-
ous! They are exuberant! They are also bewildered and
lonely.

The new Soviet regime is sorting itself out with
frequent and contradictory orders. The reins tighten
daily. No warning, no explanation.

"You think you can trust Jerzy?" Mom asks Moses.

"He's a good man, but I can't trust anyone."

"You're going in tomorrow?"

"Sure, and pretend like I'm completely stupid."

My mother, Moses, and I are still using our Aryan
names, just in case the Soviet regime decides to hate Jews
too. My mother is still Basia Siudetska, and I am Teresa
Kurek. Moses is Marian Szmorlinski. He spent the war
years hiding in a forest, hanging out with partisans, and
being part of the Russian army. He speaks Russian like a
native. He can drink like one too. And he knows how to
put on a good act of comradeship. I guess that's how he
was appointed to this position in Gdansk.

Mom first brought him to our place in Warsaw right
after they found each other among the lists of Jewish
survivors. At that time he wore a Russian army uniform,
without insignia. It's all he had. In spite of his thinness he
looked awfully handsome with his wide shoulders, V-
shaped physique, thick black wavy hair, and sapphire-
blue eyes. His stories of survival in the forests of Poland
were fascinating. I was attracted immediately. When we
walked together, I tried to match my steps to his long

powerful ones. I stretched my eight-year-old legs as far as they would go and hoped to impress him, to establish a relationship between us. "No," he instructed, "a girl must walk like a ballet dancer, toes first with a gentle shift of weight." I believed him and so I practice walking just like that whenever I have a chance.

Life seems peaceful here in Gdansk, but I do not attend school. We don't even talk about it. First we needed to settle. Then my mother fell in the snow and broke both her wrists. She needed help, of course, so it made sense that I stay home. Now that the casts are off, the doctors have told her that she must strengthen her wrists. For about two hours each day she must exercise, then drag ever-increasing weights, which are just iron bars attached to ropes. We cushion them with rags to protect our floors. As part of her workout, mom and I slide around on the floor with rags under our shoes. She is pulling the weights over our already gleaming parquet hardwood. I am just having fun.

When we are not gliding around pretending we are on an ice rink, I make doll carriages out of wooden matchboxes, glue, and some crayons. The boxes are plentiful because Mom needs the matches to light the stove and Moses needs them to light the cigarettes that he rolls with tissue paper and loose tobacco. I need the boxes to keep me occupied.

The drawer part of the matchbox makes the bed for the doll. I use the tops to cut out wheels and hoods for my carriages. When the carriages are finished and painted, I make dolls out of cardboard and doll clothing from paper. I have quite a collection of carriages with little paper dolls. Each one is individually decorated.

Unlike my mother or me, my dolls have lots of
clothing and jewelry. Some of my dolls have beads
painted on them, sometimes red ones, sometimes yellow
ones like the necklace that Mom found in a drawer of the
maple chest in the big bedroom. The amber stones of this
necklace are oval and translucent, small at the back of the
neck and gradually becoming larger toward the front.
Warm shades of yellow, gold, and brown run through
them. Some of the beads have tiny dark objects that are
little bugs. I love the way they look on Mom. Except for
the cross, it's the only jewelry I have ever seen her wear.

We guess the former occupants just forgot them in
the haste of their terror. As for us, we aren't too sure of
our situation either. The whispers that I hear tell of
strange events. They are increasing in frequency and
tension.

"Remember that nice guy, Janush, I told you about?"
Moses whispers to my Mom.

"Yeah."

"He disappeared."

"Oh my God!"

"You know what really scares me?"

"What?"

"They put two million zlotys of the company's
money in a bank under my name."

"Think they are testing you?"

"Humph! Remember Jerzy? Well, he's in prison
now—for anticommunist activities. Guess someone didn't
like him."

My mother's movements are abrupt these days.
Both she and Moses seem ever more guarded in their
conversations. They do not try to keep me from listening.
Mom is constantly doing things that don't need doing.

She opens her mouth as if she is going to tell me something, changes her mind, and then says nothing. She gets
her weights. I ask if I can help. No, she tells me, she needs
to think alone.

The snow has begun to thaw but we still hardly
ever go outside. I wish I could see the Baltic Sea but my
mother says she doesn't want to go out because she is
afraid of slipping again, and she does not want me to go
alone either.

Mom and Moses listen a lot to a radio they keep in
the kitchen under a towel. They leave it so low I can
hardly hear it. It's all news. Sometimes it's in German. I
do not understand German but they do.

I think we are moving again. It's got something to
do with all that whispering and Moses's job. Mom and
Moses pack our belongings one night. Just the minimum
stuff. He leaves this morning just as though he is just
going to the office. No luggage, no extra money. I hear
them agree that he won't take a single zloty out of that
fortune in the bank in his name. Nothing that might
arouse suspicion.

That night my mother and I wait for someone to
pick us up. Moses is not with us. I don't even know
where we are going. We are leaving just as we came, with
our coats, our hats, and three old suitcases. All the fine
china and elegant stuff in this house will be waiting for
the next occupant. All except one thing, the amber necklace Mom found in the bedroom.

It's almost evening. Darkness and quiet envelop our
world. We are waiting for the sound of a truck. Ah! There
is the quiet knock we were expecting. Here he is. We
follow our fellow a short distance, walking just like he is,
trying not to make any noise. He looks around carefully.

141

He is scared too. He whistles. The answer appears to satisfy him. We turn the corner and see a Russian army truck, covered with tarpaulin, parked in the shadow of a tree. It's a "borrowed" truck. Some money must have changed hands at a nearby depot. I understand about bribes.

He hurries us into the tarpaulin-covered back of the truck. In the brief flash of his flashlight we see other people packed tightly together with knitted brows, pursed lips, ears calculating every footstep, every motor sound. As usual, I'm the only child. Mom and I squeeze in and sit on our baggage. No one talks. We are moving.

It's just three long hours to the German border. That is where my mother says we are going. Nervous body heat keeps us sweaty warm. Snow is falling gently on the tarp roof but the roads remain passable. We are almost there, they are saying.

The guards at the German checkpoint lift an edge of the tarp as if to inspect the contents and we all freeze. They have been paid off, of course, but you never know. We hear the driver joking with the guards. The laughter is reassuring, but we are still mistrustful. My heart is knocking hard. Finally our driver starts up the truck again. There is a collective whoosh of exhalation from the crowd under the tarp.

The worst is over. So far our guides seem honest, as honest as one can expect in such situations. The snow has turned to rain. The pitter-patter on the tarp overhead is rhythmical and soothing. I drift off.

When the truck stops and I wake, it's dawn. Someone lifts the tarp and brightness floods in, washing over our gray, tired faces. Like newly hatched spiders we unwind our arms and legs, find our belongings, and get out. We are out of Poland! We have escaped the clutches of communism and arrived in the part of Berlin that is controlled by the Western powers. I don't understand the politics, but I do understand that finally, we are all safe! I too exhale a big "Yay!!"

The people are animated, talking, exchanging information. We hear Yiddish, German, Polish, Russian. Our guide points to a train station just across the way that will take most of us to displaced persons' camps in Germany.

Our suitcases are heavy. My mother takes two and I drag one. The train will take us to West Berlin, where we hope to meet Moses. He left separately to avoid suspicion. I don't know how he traveled. We pick up our baggage again as we hear the whistle of the coming train. Once inside, we ease into the luxury of real seats. At last there is another whistle; chug, chug, chug. We are moving again.

I watch as Mom's face releases some of its strain. She removes her hat and wipes the sweat off her brow. She unbuttons her coat and mine, puts them on our seats, and we both stretch. Mom smiles. She brushes the hair off my face, and then takes out her comb and lipstick.

The morning sun's golden rays splash through the window of our train and stop momentarily on the amber beads resting around my mom's neck. The insects, trapped in those golden cocoons, will never get free. But we did. Now they serve as our mementos of Gdansk, of our close escape, of our good fortune.

Leonia with her amber beads

24

Displaced Persons' Camp
Rachel, 1946

Most of us here in the displaced persons' camp in Germany consider ourselves very fortunate; we have survived. We are in a place that is safe, and our most important needs are provided for. We are in Berlin, the very capital of our persecutors, our tormentors, our murderers. No country really wants us, but Germany has no choice. It lost the war. That is why UNRA (United Nations Relief Agency), the organization set up by the United Nations to administer the problem of the refugees of World War II, set up these camps here.

We certainly are displaced—displaced out of Poland, Rumania, Hungary, Czechoslovakia, Austria, and almost every other European country. Those are the countries of our birth but no longer of our allegiance. They have betrayed us. They do not want us. We continue to escape from their disguised anti-Semitism, from creeping communism, from bitter memories of centuries of pogroms, and from the nightmare of the holocaust. We all know what we are escaping from, but there is no place to escape to. We are the untouchables of this continent. America is more eager to welcome former Nazis than us. It is apprehensive that we might have communist leanings. We have malnutrition, lice, hepatitis, scurvy, bleeding gums, missing teeth, and all sorts of nervous conditions that the doctors cannot cure.

Mom is forever scratching. Two parallel tracks of fingernail scrapes cross her back every which way she can reach. It looks like a crazy map. "Please," she asks me when Moses is not around, "scratch a little here over my rib where I cannot reach. It's driving me wild." I massage the area. I cannot bear to dig deeper over the welts that are already there. Rivulets of blood are flowing around the scabs that have formed and that have been re-scratched in the last couple of days. I dab them with cotton and alcohol. Mom seems to like the sting of the alcohol. It feels good, she says. The local physicians have tried every kind of salve and pill without any relief. From her neck down to her buttocks Mom's back is a testimony to war.

Aside from all the physical problems, we all suffer from the lack of a country of our own. We suffer from unwantedness. Doesn't anyone love us? Where is there a people or a country to welcome us? None of us wish to stay here in this concentrated ghetto in Germany. The looks we get from the local populace are hostile, even though none of them ever admits to having been a Nazi.

Like it or not, here we are. Not only that, but we are living better than the Germans. They have a shortage of everything, especially the meat and dairy items that are so dear to their palates. These are terrible times for their hausfraus, they complain. They must do without good schnitzels and eggs and butter and jams and chocolates! Only we have them. We get them free. They come to us imported from America. It's really too bad, but most of us are all out of sympathy for the Germans. If they have lots of money, some among us are willing to barter!

What would you give me for a couple pounds of butter? An Oriental rug perhaps? (Was this one stolen from us in the first place?) Some fine jewelry? An antique vase your soldiers brought back from the Jewish homes they pilfered? A set of fine bone Rosenthal china? All is fair in love and war, and now the tables have turned; not sufficiently for us, but nicely.

So yes, we have the butter. Eggs and milk too, although they come in powdered form. UNRA packages arrive daily at our camps, filled with these wonderful things from America. Those in charge of the food supplies, like my stepfather, Moses, could easily get some extra provisions to trade for valuable items. But if we trade a stick of butter for a beautiful candelabrum, how can we be sure that the blood of the original Jewish owner will not haunt us forever? Some take advantage. Not Moses. He won't sell his soul, or ours, for a trinket. He has lost his first wife and daughter; everything but his integrity. Mom and I are proud of him.

We are alive. We have food. We have our self-respect. We own nothing else. Everything we possess fits into the same three suitcases we smuggled out of Poland. "To hell with profiteering. Give those German bastards anything but poison?" Not Moses! Not us!

Our room has one table and two beds—actually, one bed and a cot for me. Living in close quarters means that there is no privacy. If Mom and Moses don't want me to know something, they discuss it in Yiddish. They do so late at night when they believe I am asleep. My eyes are closed but I'm not asleep, and I listen very carefully, especially if I hear my name mentioned. I'm beginning to understand a lot. (Tip to language teachers: Pretend to have secrets in the language your students cannot understand. Let their name pop up here and there. You need do nothing else. It's like a language pill. I guarantee amazing results.)

The daily topic all over the camp is everyone's pending emigration. There is no reason to hide whatever is going on from us children. We hear it all even if we do not understand all the implications.

"Did you hear that twelve-year-old Jasha Anhalt has a cousin in Argentina? UNRA found her. Thank goodness she has at least one living relative in this world."

"Do you know that America has cut its quota for Polish-born people?"

"What are the requirements for applying to Brazil?"

"What are the chances of getting past the British if you try to smuggle into Haifa?"

"Did you hear over fifty Polish Jews were murdered when they tried to repossess their former homes in Kielce, Poland?"

It has been over a year, and we still have no place to go. The British are reneging on their promises to the Jews. They are more concerned now with befriending the Arabs because of the oil in those lands. Will world compassion or guilt ensure that Israel is established? Can't count on that. Other than Israel, America is our goal, but America has its own agenda. The U.S. is fearful that Eastern European Jews will be undesirables, such as communists and unskilled workers. Marx was Jewish; Lenin too. Those types are definitely unwelcome. Not even the Statue of Liberty is ready for the tired, the poor, the wretched refuse of Europe and its wars! An exception is made for Germans, especially if they are scientists, even Nazi scientists. Justice has its limits.

Many of us came here with only false papers, or no papers. We have names and dates that never existed before the war. We are used to finagling. Now we must decide who we really want to be.

"What do you think? Should I declare German birth or Rumanian birth?"

"I heard from my cousin in Chicago and she said that America is looking for scientists. Can you say you are an engineer?"

"Don't ever mention a handicap. Try to hide it. If your have a disability, you may not find any country willing to take you in."

A joke going around has an immigrant going to a rabbi and asking whether it would be best to declare his son's age a year younger or a year older than he really is. The rabbi suggests, "Why not declare his real age?" The immigrant looks at him awestruck, "Thank you, Rabbi, I would never have thought of that!"

Mom and Moses decide that if America prefers those of German birth, we will be German-born. Moses declares that we were all born in Oels, a small village on the border between Germany and Poland, where records were destroyed. That is an important piece of research, since in reality none of us has ever heard of this place. Small towns where bureaus of statistics went up in smoke will not contest our word. They are acquiring large numbers of previously unknown births. But who can argue?

To get entrance visas, we need relatives who will pay for our passage and guarantee that we will not be welfare burdens. Mom has an uncle in New York, her mother's brother, Joseph Richland. She also has a brother, Leon Honigstein, in Brazil. UNRA found them. They must each put up the money for our journey. We apply for entrance into both countries. Whoever takes us first can have us. All we do now is wait.

We wait six months in the first DP camp and then we are transferred to another one, also in Berlin. They are almost identical, as far as I can see. Same type of barracks, same type of food from UNRA, same bathhouses with huge shower rooms where dozens of bodies are soaping and rinsing themselves with nary a thought of embarrassment. No curtains anywhere. Here are all shapes of women: thin women, fat women, pregnant women, disfigured women, even a dwarf. There are adolescents and pubescent children. Only the old, over fifty, are missing. They were vaporized in the "showers" of Auschwitz and other concentration camps.

I am aghast. I don't want to stare at these laughing and gossiping women so completely unconcerned about their breasts and their bellies. They have genital hair too. I have never seen such nakedness. The lessons of the convent are still with me. There, we dared not even look at our own bodies below the waist. Here, I don't know where not to look first. I seem to be the only skinny, breastless eight-year-old girl to be so self-conscious.

Outdoors there is excitement in the bustling groups of kids that congregate in the alleys between the barracks. I love to listen to the many conversations in various languages.

"Where are you from?"

"From Kiev." "From Budapest." "From Rumania."

"How did you survive?"

"We hid in a cellar for two years." "We escaped to Russia." "I was rescued from Auschwitz."

"Where will you be going?"

"Israel." "America." "Cuba." "South Africa."

"Do you have any family?"

"UNRA is trying to find them."

Schools seem to have materialized overnight. Some committee has decided that all the kids will be taught in Hebrew, the language known to none of us. No one grumbles or requests Hebrew second-language tutors. For most of us it is already our third or fourth language, so Hebrew is not really a problem, and it is certainly equal opportunity for all. At first I do not understand a single word except for the numbers that are written on the board. Some of the people who have been here longer are more familiar with this language. They become teachers' helpers. I love school. It makes me feel important. It is my first experience of regular attendance.

The alphabet is unlike any I have ever seen. It is written backwards. Stick pictures tell us that "*yalda*" is a girl, "*yeled*" a boy. They also identify "mother," "father," "table," "bread." Within six months, like most of the kids, I manage rudimentary Hebrew vocabulary. Moses enjoys helping me. He spent a few years in Palestine as a youth and speaks it fluently. After all, when and if Israel becomes a reality, that will be our people's language.

Sometimes school provides trips. If it is not too far, we march to get there. We form long columns of about three or four abreast as we thread together down the middle of the streets. We yell in Hebrew, "*Ahat, ahat, ahat shtaim shalosh arba. Ahat, ahat,*" etc. meaning "one, two, three, four." The louder the better. We, the Jewish youth, well fed at last, marching with arrogant abandon through the rubble of Berlin. Germans watch. They are not smiling.

I hear that some of the older girls, like twelve or thirteen, sneak out and go to a pub. They think they are very clever. I think they are too. They wear lipstick and they smoke and they order beer. I try that too. How can they stand that strong, dark German brew? I almost choke to death as the awful bitterness attacks my taste buds and then slowly slides down my esophagus, later to evaporate through every pore of my body. That is how my mother finds out about it. She says that I stink. She tells me not to associate with those girls anymore. I feel awful too. But I still resist a little because I want to be like those smart older girls.

Food here in our camp is good enough and sufficient, but my legs are still bowed and my gums bleed all the time. A physician decides that the best therapy for me is the new X-ray treatment available at the local clinic where we can go, just two stops away on the trolley. Of course I can do it. I go there all by myself once a week, and it doesn't hurt a bit. They put two pads next to each cheekbone, there is a little buzz, and that is all. There is nothing to it. The trolley stops right in front of the clinic and it lets me off right in front of our DP camp.

Several weeks pass without any problems. Then one day while at the clinic I recognize Vera, another patient from our camp. She is older than I, and I am surprised that her mom comes with her. Perhaps it is only because it is her first time. Her mom asks me if she could come home with me since I know the way. Oh sure, I proudly assure the mom.

After our treatments Vera and I walk to the station and board the trolley. Two stops. They seem longer than usual, but I counted them carefully. We exit. What strange terrain. These are not the familiar streets I expect. Where is the camp? Had I miscounted? Neither of us has any money, nor can we speak German. It can't be far. We decide to walk.

We wander for hours. *"Wie is das Juden camp?"* we try asking. Some don't answer. Some point. Some talk a whole lot but we understand nothing. It's getting darker and rain is drizzling. I'm terrified, especially because I have a responsibility. I must maintain a brave face in front of her. Our shoes are soaked and our toes are frozen. Our teeth are chattering.

Dusk becomes dark. Not too many people on the street. Did vengeful Berliners misdirect us on purpose? Every shadow is suspect. Every noise might be a Nazi.

I feel my Jewishness here. My vulnerably in a hostile world. This constant need to hide who I really am. At the DP camp, where I am surrounded by other Jews, I don't worry about my safety. Some are nice and others are not so nice, but all of them are Jewish. All of them are like my extended family. I feel sure that none of them would hurt me. It is the first time in my memory that I feel free. I feel proud. I have taken off my cross.

Right now both Vera and I fervently hope that they are looking for us. They must be alarmed. I know I will be held responsible for this if we ever get back. Perhaps I'll even be punished. But I know that will not be fatal. What I am really scared of is what will happen if they do not find us quickly. I have heard the stories of many children who survived terrible ordeals. My imagination fills each dreadful moment with pictures of lingering Nazis waiting for the right moment to grab us and to torment us. Will the adults save us in time? Will we be found before we are dead?

We plaster ourselves against the wall of a building trying to find shelter. We are both shaking with terror,

Rachel, 1946

each afraid to even admit to the other how scared we are. It seems forever before we hear the wonderful sound of our own names being called, "Rachel, Vera!!" These are our own people calling us, the DP police. They care. They have a car. What a great relief!

No one had ever mentioned to me that more than one trolley can run on the same track, and that they do not all go to the same place. Mom did not know that either! So it really wasn't my fault.

Back in this wonderful DP camp I see my first movie ever. It is *Little Black Sambo*. It's that cartoon representation of Negroes, black as coal, huge saucer eyes, and magnificent super-white teeth that light up perpetual smiles on huge lips. Then one day, as my mother and I are walking, I see the real thing, a black GI. I run ahead to follow him stealthily, hoping to get a frontal view. Finally I get it. What a surprise. Where are those oversize white teeth and huge lookers? Where is that shiny, bitter-chocolate skin? I am so confused. Somewhere Mom borrows a copy of *Uncle Tom's Cabin*. We read it together. So … I realize we are not the only people singled out for mistreatment! My heart goes out to the Negroes.

Rochelle Dreeben

Our next film, *The Search*, is about a mother and a young boy who search long and hard for each other after the war. They traipse through many places, almost meeting but somehow always missing each other over and over again. Their ending is a happy one.

I try to conjure up my own father's face. It has been more than three years since he lifted me over the wall of the ghetto. I wonder, *Isn't it possible that one day my real father might find us? Miracles happen. He might be alive!*

There is a song that the kids sing here in the DP camp. It sticks with me like no other. Although it's in Polish, it's a Jewish song.

Once there were tangos, foxtrots, and waltzes
Sung during enchanting times;
And then there were words, of yearning and nostalgia,
That brought out resentment in our hearts:
Tango of the prisoner, reminds us of our suffering,
Tango of the prisoner, of our days in Auschwitz,
Bayonets of steel, and the guards' rigid faces
For freedom we yearn, of freedom we dream,
Until that moment when our chains are broken
And the agony in our breast is released
My lips will murmur:
Tango of the prisoner.
When our days of rejoicing return.
Let a Negro play his saxophone
And the rhythm in his music unite us all.
Let an Englishman and Frenchman
Sing their chant of lasting peace
And once again will come our days of joy.

25

No Choice
Leonia, Fall 1946

The handsome young doctor at the Berlin clinic greets me with his customary German smile. He has been treating me for months for a tenacious itch on my back. "Good morning, Mrs. Schleifstein. Please tell me if the salve that I have prescribed for you is effective?" Then he looks at my back, and stops smiling "Why, it is very bad, terrible. Your back still looks like a bloody railroad depot. If you want these scars ever to heal you must stop this scratching!"

Yes, I'm thinking. Like the bloody tracks that your people used to transport my people to their death. My nerves cannot heal so fast. Your little salve isn't that potent. I try to rationalize. He is young, probably totally innocent. Yes, but so were all those children sent to their death on those tracks. He is still a German. I'm still a Jew. His touch defiles me. But this is the only medical facility that is open to me. I need his knowledge. Also I must have the answer to the test I had last week. It's not my back that concerns me most at this moment. It's that I suspect I might be pregnant. I'm hoping that I am wrong and dreading the possibility that the answer is *yes*.

"Don't worry," he tells me. "We will try another salve, and maybe some vitamins as well. The good news is that you're healthy otherwise." Now he smiles a really big grin. "Oh, and the best news is that yes, you are pregnant!"

I feel like a bomb just hit me. Without a home, without a country, and pregnant. How can this be? I haven't had a period for over two years, not since the burning of the Warsaw Ghetto. I'm the weakling who was told by the doctor that delivered Rachel that I'd never be able to have another child. I'm almost forty years old. What shall I do?

When I get back to our room, Moses is there, obviously just after a bath. I can smell the scent of the American soap we have been using. His bushy, black, curly hair has been carefully groomed and caged in a special hair net for men. He emanates vitality. We have never discussed having children. He lost his wife and only daughter in the war and I have no idea how he might react. It's a total surprise to him. Yet his reaction is instant.

His face lights up. A joyful smile plays around his open lips. I need no further clue. He is in some fairyland, in total denial of our situation.

He anticipates this new child with a conviction that I lack. He has no doubt that we can do it. I watch as he paces excitedly back and forth in our single room, the smile never leaving his face. Dreams wash over him. A new life, perhaps a son of his own! A child to fulfill his aspirations, his longings for a family, someone to continue his line. His hopes are boundless.

"Leonia, this is a time to celebrate!" he declares as he gets two glasses and a bottle of his favorite 140-proof Russian vodka. He hands one glass to me. I take a small sip. I force myself to drink it all up. It burns my tongue and my throat but does not alleviate my concerns. Nor does it cause a miscarriage.

"But we are still just vagrants," I agonize. "We have nothing to give this child and don't even know where or when we might finally be allowed to make a home. And I don't have the strength of a young person."

Moses squares his wide shoulders. His V-shaped physique looks young and agile. "Look at me, I'm only forty-two years old, still young enough to earn us a living. His blue eyes are sparkling with confidence as he continues to reassure me. "You are still young too, plenty young enough to have this baby. This one is a miracle for which we must be grateful."

I sit there numb. An infant in this inhospitable country that despises us as we despise it. In spite of Moses's enthusiasm I'm not convinced. I do not want this added burden at this uncertain time. This is not the place to have a baby. Yet this new life must have a chance. I cannot abort. Whatever happens, I cannot allow a German hand to kill another Jewish child.

26

Paris

Rachel, Spring 1947

Both Mom and Moses are very busy. They are packing, so I guess we are moving again. There on their bed are the three suitcases that we have dragged from Warsaw to Gdansk, to our original place in the displaced persons camp in Berlin, and then to the second one, also in Berlin, where we have been less than four months. I know the signs well. The only thing I don't know is where we are going this time. Well, maybe if I just stand there long enough, somebody will tell me something. Finally Mom looks up at me and she knows right away what I want.

"Guess what Rachel, we have some great news."

"Oh?"

"We're going to Paris! Yes, we are taking a train to go there next Wednesday. Isn't that exciting?"

"I thought we were waiting to go to America."

"Well, UNRA found Moses's older sister Manya and her husband Sam Urviez. They are family. They had emigrated from Poland to France before the war, and survived there. Now they have agreed to house us. So we can stay there until we get a visa to the U.S."

I had no idea that we had family there, and of course Paris does sound glamorous. On the other hand,

*Leonia in a high hat and Rachel in her beret (left).
On right, Max Urviez (son of Manya and Sam
Urviez), his wife and their son, Guillaume. At the
entrance to a park in Paris, 1946.*

I'm just barely adjusted to this place. Oh well! Another year, another city, another language, another school. But I really am excited.

*****

I'm wearing a beret now just like all the French people. And I can speak a little in French, very little. But already I have been to the Eiffel Tower, and I have walked on the famous Champs Elysées, and I know where the famous Louvre is, and we have been riding on the subway where they have maps of all the routes. All you have to do is press a button to show at what station you are standing, and then another where you want to go, and the route lights up with little electric lights. I bet I wouldn't get lost here like I did in Berlin. I hope Mom will let me go somewhere by myself one day. I feel very cosmopolitan. If we wind up going to still another country, I'll be able to boast about my adventures in beautiful Paris. I wonder if that will help me impress some friends. Sure hope so.

Manya and Sam are really old. But after a few minutes their wrinkles don't matter, because they are so warm and energetic. When we first came here a lot of the family came to meet us at the station. It took me a while to figure out who is who. After all, they have four sons and three daughters and a lot of grandchildren—that's a lot of people and names to remember. I stood there while they were all hugging and kissing and talking at the same time. At first I thought that they were only Moses's family. But now Mom tells me that they are related to us as well as to Moses. That is because before the war, Manya's sister was married to my mother's brother. Mom still remembers that wedding, when they were all there together and Manya said, 'I hope you'll come visit me in Paris one day. You'll always be welcome in our house." Of course, that was before the war and before I was born.

Paris really is beautiful, but not particularly so where we live with Manya and Sam. Their place is pretty small. The main room has a big table, chairs, and a small cot for me to sleep on. It adjoins an alcove with a small icebox, a sink, and some burners. All the clean dishes are stacked under the sink behind a curtain. Two other small rooms are used as bedrooms. There is no bathroom inside the apartment. Everyone has to wait his or her turn to use the toilet or the bathing room down the hall. We share them with several other apartments. In the morning they are both very busy. Doors open and slam shut to check if one of them is free. There's a lot of moaning and groaning and always someone with clenched teeth muttering, "Merde," as though that might help.

Mom and Manya really like one another. They have a past that they can share. Manya is old and Mom is pregnant so they try to outdo each other in helpfulness. Like when we are eating, Mom sometimes takes the plates away even before we're finished. Everybody laughs, especially Sam. He talks very little, just smiles or nods in agreement. He is always cold, and he complains sometimes about the draftiness in the apartment and about the poor quality of the building and everything else nowadays. But he is so pleasant and agreeable that we all like him. He likes to wear old, comfortable clothes—usually a flannel shirt and baggy pants, that look like he dragged them out of a pile of rags. His sons say, "So Dad, are these pants the latest style among the 'rag people?'" Sam never minds the teasing. He just laughs. Of course we all know that buying and selling rags was his business all his life. He gave up that business to one of his daughters, Rose, and her husband, but he still enjoys going over there to help out.

I call him "Grandpa Sam" just like all his real grandkids do, and I think he likes it. When Sam and I are alone he teaches me to play cards and checkers. Sometimes he lets me win. But what I look forward to the most are visits with Sam to his old house and rag yard where his daughter Rose and granddaughter, Lillian, live. She is my age and my idol. If I could make my hair curl in ringlets like hers, and have these tiny light brown wisps all around my forehead, I would be so happy. Lillian is smart and funny and everybody loves her. I think she has a little lisp, but then maybe that is the right way to speak French. I try to copy that. My mom doesn't think it's so funny, but I think it's cute. And Mom doesn't speak French either so she does not know. I understand a lot already, though I don't have enough words. But things are improving. I understand a lot more now. Lillian is the only girl among all her boy cousins so she is sort of the princess. Whatever it is that Lillian does, it is wonderful. Like last week, Lillian got a great report card and everyone drooled about how smart she is. Well, I think she is too. But in my family nobody makes a big fuss over good grades. They just expect it. In fact, when my teacher promoted me to the next level, because she said that my French has improved so much, no one said I was smart.

There is even a piano in Lillian's house. She shows me how to play one easy song and hopefully I will learn more. That is the best thrill of all. I would really like to just be left alone with the piano for a couple of hours. But I would not ask. So I practice a lot in my head and finger imaginary piano notes on my knees. It's almost like the real thing. But what I would really like is to be talented like Lillian's uncle Richard. He never took any lessons. He just sits down at the piano and plays. We just ask for a song and there it is. They call it playing by ear. That is really a wonderful talent. When Lillian and I sing songs that we make up, we try to outdo each other with higher and higher notes until we are both screeching. Her mom is so good, she never even hollers or gets mad at us for making all that noise. It's so easy to be comfortable there.

*Rachel with Pierre and Guillaume Urviez on
Paris Rooftop, 1946.*

Even though Grandpa Sam's place is so small, all
the family likes to come here on Sundays. How we manage to fit there on cold rainy days is amazing. Grandma
Manya and Sam go out and buy a lot of wine and cold
cuts and the long French baguettes that are so delicious.
They take me along to help them carry all the stuff home.
Actually, I have a hard time keeping from eating those
baguettes immediately. Their smell is so tempting. But I
must behave and resist. It's not like it was when we were
in the ghetto. I know I will be allowed to eat all I want
when the company comes.

Manya and Sam have seven children and a lot of
grandchildren. The apartment fills up quickly. After the
customary double-kiss greeting, the adults gather around
the table. The rest of us find a spot anywhere we can,
around it or under it. We fill our plates. The coffee smells
delicious. Before you know it the place is jammed and
conversation just takes off.

Rochelle Dreeben

Everyone seems to want to talk at once. It's almost always politics. During the war, two of Manya's sons were in the French resistance. They cut telephone lines, carried messages, and tried to blow up trains carrying German troops. It was their policy to make sure that any stray German soldier they caught should disappear. But now they argue a lot regarding the communists. Are they good or are they bad for France? The discussions get pretty heated. They are usually in both French and Jewish so that Moses can participate too. He had worked for the communists when we were in Gdansk after the war, so he claims firsthand experience. He thinks one cannot trust them. That was why we had to escape from there. But Max, the eldest son, is never convinced. He keeps talking about the poor people in France and that only a communist government would help them get a better life. Manya and Sam say very little except to hush everyone now and then. "Peace, peace, our neighbors will be upset," they plead. And for a very brief while the voices tone down somewhat.

We kids often listen even when we don't intend to do it, and somehow we do understand a lot even when some of the conversation doesn't make sense.

After the lunch, as soon as the table gets cleared, out come the cigarettes. The men roll up tobacco in special thin papers and light up. They huff and puff for a while as the air in the room changes color and loses transparency. It's hot and hazy. It really smells awful. The men don't care. They're ready for poker. Someone shuffles the cards. Politics recede. The game begins.

From the women I learn some of the family stories. Fela, the eldest daughter, lost her husband in the French army. He was captured as a French soldier, but never returned, killed as a prisoner because he was Jewish. She now lives with a very nice man whom she cannot marry. If she did, she would lose two pensions, one from the French government and the other from the Germans. Nobody cares about this arrangement. This is France.

I love Sundays. I always hope that Lillian will come and that the weather will be good enough so that we can persuade the grownups to take us to the Bois de Boulogne. That is the best place to be. The oaks there are huge and just budding; the paths zigzag so that it's fun to run on them or to hide from each other behind the evergreens. They smell wonderful in every part of the park. If we can get a boat ride in one of the lakes, or a carousel ride, it's special. That costs money, so we don't ask often.

Mom loves the Bois too. But she also likes all the other places, like the Champs Elysées or the area around the Louvre. Her stomach is getting pretty big and heavy so we go to places where there are benches to sit on. The grown-ups share stories and jokes and have a good time. "That's how it used to be before the war," Mom tells me. "Lots of company and relatives. I was never alone."

My school is a large building divided by a wall that separates the boys from the girls. Even the play yard is divided. During recess a lot of the older girls stand on tiptoes near the dividing wall and try to make conversation with the boys on the other side. They vie with each other for the best place near the small hole in that wall. They are very silly. The rest of us play jump rope or try to climb a pole. It's hard. I cannot do it. There is no other equipment for recess fun. But I do pretty well in the classroom. The way it works here is that your place in the class is your mark. Whenever I get to be the first, second, or third out of about twenty-five I'm advanced to the next level. I have already skipped twice, as my French got better. But I don't know what grade I'm in, and I haven't made any friends.

Fridays are "lice days." Each of us has to shower in school and wash her hair with special soap. That is because many students come from homes without bath facilities. Lice inspection follows. My mother has been combing the creatures out of my hair ever since she found me back in Poland, so I'm lice-free. But it is a constant struggle.

There is a girl a little smaller than I am that I often pass on the way to school. She is skimpily dressed in grimy, unmended, un-ironed clothes. She is usually alone, although sometimes I see her taking care of a very young baby just as dirty as she is. I have the feeling that she is hungry, and I know she does not go to school. She has an angry look about her so I avoid eye contact, but one day she throws a stone at me. It lands right above my left eyebrow and leaves a permanent scar. "Dirty Jew" she yells as I run away. She knows nothing about me except that I am cared for, and she is not.

When our company arrives the following Sunday, they ask how I got hurt, and I tell them about this girl.

"See," Max says, "that is why we need a communist government. Too many of our children are neglected like that. The parents are not educated; they have too many kids and not enough income. They can barely provide a roof and some food."

The arguments start all over again.

27

Henry
Rachel, April 1947

In April, Mom disappears for a whole week into the hospital and then comes back with baby Henry. All the relatives goo-goo and make a big fuss over him, but Mom just keeps pointing out that he has a normal thumb, not like her thumb. They look puzzled. Only Manya seems to understand. She knows the stories about the Honigstein

Moses   *Leonia*
Paris, 1947

thumb. She brings Mom a beautiful ruby necklace and says, "This is a necklace that goes back several generations in our family. I want you to have it now and enjoy it in good health. That is part of our tradition." Mom takes

Manya's hand and holds it a long time, then puts on that necklace. She wears it a lot. I think it really gives her joy.

The little apartment is suddenly much smaller. The baby's needs are all around. There are diapers hanging everywhere. The tiny kitchen is always busy with something for the baby. When the Jewish Agency gives us an opportunity to move into a room in the country, Mom and Moses seem very happy about it. They are concerned that Manya and Sam need to regain their own space, that they have neither peace nor privacy while we live with them. I know I will miss Paris and our French family, especially Lillian. I do not want to leave.

28

Memories

Leonia, Prewar

We're in La Croix St. Ouen, a tiny village set in a beautiful country area a couple of hours north of Paris. There are only two children here, and even they are not Rachel's age. She is bored.

"Oh, it's raining!" she moans. "What shall I do today?" Rachel is glum as she looks out our window. The pervasive clouds are getting darker by the minute. I'm tempted to say, "So why don't you chase some flies and catch them." That's what my own mother would have said. On the other hand if I had posed that same question to my father, he would probably crook his neck in mock sympathy, look at me with a twinkle in his eye, caress his short, soft, well-groomed beard, then say something like, "Would you like to know what a young girl in a very difficult situation like yours might have done had she lived in Spain two hundred years ago?

I would know immediately that a story was coming. And no one was a better storyteller than my father. He would start off speaking slowly and steadily, perhaps outlining the paragraphs in his own mind. His voice was low and even. I would look for a comfortable spot to sit at his knees or at the table in anticipation of an exciting adventure. Before long some of my brothers or friends would be listening too. Even my mother would find a place to listen once again to the magic of his tales. We would soon be fully involved in a history lesson that came alive for us as though it were a movie. There were heroes and heroines and good kings and wicked people, and it didn't matter if we had already heard a similar story before. Our hearts were beating in the parts where there was a danger or a problem for our heroes. Each storytelling was fresh and exciting. The rainy afternoon would melt away like a brief summer shower, leaving only its own sweet aftertaste.

Our father, Chaim David, was the youngest of nine children. His own father died before I was born so I didn't know him. But I did know his mother, who was my grandmother Rachel Dziedzic Honigstein. She chose to live with her favorite son, so we were lucky to have her in our home. Even though we had a live-in maid, it was only when Grandma Rachel was in our home that everything ran smoothly. When she left occasionally to spend some time in one of her other children's homes, our place became a disaster. Dust gathered. Nothing could be found. Meals deteriorated. The maid was at a loss about what to do. So was my mother. She candidly admitted that she had no talent for housekeeping and was just as anxious as the rest of us to have Grandma Rachel take over that responsibility. "When is Grandma Rachel coming back?" was on everybody's mind. She managed it all with efficiency and good-natured patience. We all loved her a lot. That is why I named my Rachel after her.

Our mother, Chaya Richland, a beauty from a much wealthier background than that of our father, was petite and pretty and very coquettish. Her thick, naturally blond hair was always stylishly arranged in braids or locks. She loved to sing and to dance and to go to parties wearing fine clothes and to have lots of company. She was always ready for company with a great welcoming smile punctuated by her famous dimples. Even though she didn't finish high school and seemed to have little interest in reading anything, I have to give her credit for being a very smart lady. Otherwise how could she have gotten my father to marry her and to adore her all her life? Nor was there any question about how much she adored him. Whenever he came home she was there with open arms, ready to embrace her husband whom she always called "my Chaim David" as though someone might want to steal him. We children laughed. I think we were even jealous.

Really they were total opposites. Our father treasured education above all. When he was young he studied to become a rabbi. I'm not sure why, but by the time I was born he was in the business of fabricating and selling leather goods like purses and wallets and belts. We were quite comfortable, at least during peacetime. But what made our home wonderful had nothing to do with money.

It was the people who loved to gather there, and we all knew who the magnet was. A relative from another town, some friends of my six brothers, or a businessman to see my father—there was always room for another chair at the massive table in the main room. Everyone interested my father. If a salesman dropped in, Dad was full of questions. "How were your sales? Did you visit the synagogue? What's the news in that town? What's going on in the political situation there? Who invited you for Shabbat dinner? What, no one? How shameful!"

The conversation would segue from business to travel to ethics or history. Often my brothers and I hung around to make sure we didn't miss anything. At the very least, there was sure to be a funny story. Everyone knew a joke about Chelm, a small town reputed to have the dumbest of people. "I heard there is a new trend in Chelm. Anybody know why everyone there is going to a dentist?" The salesman would pause to let everyone have a guess. "No? Well they are tired of being stupid. They want their wisdom teeth put back in."

Dad loved to laugh with total abandon. He would shake his arms and his chest would heave and his face would get all crinkled up. He was there, completely in the moment, enjoying whatever it was—trivia going on between himself and some youngsters, or the not so young; a serious matter would absorb him just as completely. He managed to make each person feel important. Each of us thought we were his favorite, or tried to be; so much so that a disappointed look from him devastated us. Our memories were filled only with the games he played with us, the laughter we shared, or the learning that he made interesting for us.

Of course among my six brothers and me there were plenty of fights. My father had to be a regular Solomon to sort out their mischief. With the four younger boys, it was "who kicked whom first under the table," or "where is Jerzyk," or "who swiped little Adam's dessert when he wasn't looking." If my two oldest brothers, Leon and Heniek, both had a date that evening, whose turn was it to wear the elegant new jacket? Or where were Julek's pants, which he had so carefully inserted under the mattress on the bed he shared with Ignac? He had placed them there so they would have a nice crease for the weekend. He wanted to look nice for the theater. Who took them? What about the history report that Jerzyk had left on the hall table? He needed it for school and his grade depended on it. We all knew that without top grades a Jewish boy would never be admitted to public high school,

I can still see my Mom. Discipline is no more her talent than housekeeping. She is screaming that the fighting must stop and who started it and there must be peace! Of course no one is forthcoming. And the table must be set for dinner. And Grandma Rachel is not home. And the maid refuses to do anything in all that hoopla. She stands there with her hands on her hips, acting as if she really is going to do something. But no one is paying much attention. The boys are running around the table playing "gotcha." Paper is flying all over the room. They are all howling and laughing except for little Jerzyk, who is crying in the corner because they took away his paper airplane and they are throwing it around and now it is destroyed. Jerzyk's wailing is getting no sympathy.

Suddenly my father comes in. He looks around unperturbed at the chaos as though all is perfectly normal. As he hugs his wife he pats her back and reassures her, "Hayele, my dear, don't you worry. This room will be perfect in two minutes." He looks around at the boys, assumes the voice that means business, and demands, "Boys, straighten the chairs, put away your shoes where they belong and pick up all the wads of trash off the floor. Leonia, help your mom. Then you all better wash up. You have three minutes to do it." Then he takes out his famous pocket watch with the hands that count minutes and even seconds, and starts counting. There is excitement and authority in his voice. Just as he promised, a few minutes later the room is tidy. Nobody is mad. A bunch of partly washed faces are sitting down.

Whenever I tell Rachel any of these stories, she says, "I wish I knew him and all your brothers." I feel sad that she will never remember a grandfather, especially such a good one. He was a real *mench*.

"One time I was walking with my dad and he pulled at me to cross the street. When I protested, knowing our destination was on this side, he said, 'See that old man coming our way? I loaned him some money quite a while ago. I know that he is very poor and can't repay me. If he sees us, it will only add to all his problems. I don't want him to feel humiliated.'"

When I tell Rachel that story she asks, "Mom, was that during the war?"

"It was very early in the war. Even then all the Jews were having a hard time. We had already lost everything, but my father still tried to put the best face on what had happened. When the Germans hauled away all the leather material from his shop and all the ready-made purses, wallets, and belts as well, he tried to make light of it. He thought that it would be like the First World War. 'We managed then and somehow we will do this again,' he said. I remember him exclaiming, 'Children, look how rich we were. We would never even have known our own wealth had we not seen how much stuff the Germans took away from us.'"

"In 1935, two of my older brothers were already married and had children. It was certainly my turn. My mother was always saying to me, 'Leonia, you better not expect to find anyone as wonderful as my Chaim David. They only made one of him, and I am afraid you will be looking until you're an old maid.'"

Rachel wants to know if I was really worried. Of course I was.

"It really wasn't funny. I was twenty-seven years old. I was afraid my Mom might be right. I did compare all the men I met to my father. Luckily, one day when I was helping in my father's store, your dad came in to buy a purse for his sister, and before he left we had arranged our first date. It was evident to me that he was a real family man, caring and hardworking, and he had a nice sense of humor. We laughed a lot together. I still remember the crazy movie we saw that night. It was about Charlie Chaplin and machines that did everything. They stuffed a meal into his mouth. A toothbrush appeared, all laden with paste and ready to do its job. A wet napkin slapped itself across his face and a small towel followed. Finally a brush wiped off the crumbs from his shoulders. Now he was done. So efficient! We marveled at the good life that automation would bring to the future."

Leonia as a young woman

29

Honigstein Thumbs
Leonia, Prewar

Our room inside a beautiful mansion in La Croix St. Ouen overlooks a huge but neglected lawn. Behind the house the river Oise runs toward the Seine. Best of all, Adam, my mother's brother, and his wife, Meriam, are

*Lillian and Rachel in
La Croix St. Ouen, 1947*

Meriam Honigstein, Leonia, and Moses with
Baby Henry in La Croix St. Ouen, 1947

here too. When we left them in Warsaw we didn't know
when we might meet next. This is a great surprise to me.
We are with family again.

Mom, Moses, Adam, and Meriam often spend hours
sitting outside around the huge oak tree, just talking and
talking. This afternoon it is just Mom and I and baby
Henry sleeping next to us in his carriage. I'm glad to have
this time with her alone. I watch as Mom's thumbs are
swirling around each other. They look like they are in a
mad whirl. Mom's not even aware of what her thumbs
are doing. Each seems so determined to be on top. They
are funny-looking thumbs, thick, ugly, and strong. I look
at my own thumbs, nothing special, but at least they are
perfectly normal. I guess Mom must know what I am

177

thinking. She says, "Did I ever tell you the story about the Honigstein thumb?" I know what she means because when Henry was born, she made a big deal about his thumbs. They too are just plain normal ones like mine.

"Does it have something to do with why you are always twiddling them?" I ask.

She looks at her thumbs and laughs. Two dimples appear in her cheeks. I like to see her that way. I like to hear her stories.

"These thumbs have been common in our family for generations. We think of them as an inheritance, a tradition. Without these thumbs, I wonder if we would have survived the war?" Mom's left eyebrow lifts slightly as she holds up her thumbs for my better inspection. I take another look at her magic marvels. They are like oval mushrooms, large misshapen heads on fat stunted stems. The nails seem to be growing sideways. They look like they belong to a different species. Maybe they really do have some magic.

"They are very special thumbs," she goes on. "I think of them as my lucky Honigstein thumbs. Just think, my brothers Adam, whom you know, and Leon, who is in Brazil, have these thumbs, as does my cousin Sophia in Israel; and we are the only ones from our family that survived the war. That is incredible luck! I must admit that in my younger days I didn't think they were so enviable. Still, the family always did make a big deal about them and they were the focus for a lot of jokes and mirth."

"Like how?"

"For instance, every new baby had to have a thumb inspection. That was tradition. Each uncle and aunt had to open up the tiny newborn palm and check it out. If the baby had a normal thumb, they yelled 'mazel tov!' of course. But if it had a thumb like mine, they howled, 'Double mazel tov! The Honigstein thumb lives on!' They insisted it was a living family insignia, a sign of future greatness, an oracle of sorts, a declaration of our continuity. Of course when we were in Paris, Moses's family didn't have this tradition so they didn't make much of a to-do about Henry's plain old thumbs." Mom shrugs her shoulder and laughs. "I must admit that I kind of missed the fun of it."

"So you think that those thumbs have some magic?" I ask.

"It's possible." Her face takes on a semi-serious look, waiting for me to prod her.

"So how do you account for that?"

"I can't. But I will tell you some of the stories associated with the Honigstein thumbs.

"According to my Uncle Hillel, my father's most unattractive brother, who was short, bald, and had large bulbous red nose on a pockmarked face, it all started in the nineteenth century when Russian scouts were looking for the tallest and most handsome men for the Czar's army. They kidnapped young boys whose looks pleased them. Uncle Hillel would then take on a regal posture as though he were seven feet tall, perk up his mustache, and claim that the only thing that saved him from those Russian scouts was his less-than-perfect thumbs. He never cracked a smile as he insisted that otherwise, given his remarkable good looks and incredible charm, they would certainly have grabbed him. Then he lifted one of his thumbs as though to salute it, and exclaimed, 'Thank you, God, for this wonderful gift which kept me out of the Czar's clutches.' He was only half joking. Everyone in the family knew that Great-grandfather Honigstein had been abducted in just that way as a lad, and was absent from his family for twenty years."

"Did your father, Chaim David, have those thumbs?" I ask.

"Oh yes! And so did one of his sisters and her daughter, my cousin Sofia. Did I ever tell you her story?"

"No, so what happened to her?"

"Well, she was a real character. Nothing could stop Sofia. Not her parents, not her thumbs, not any concern for whatever others thought. She was smart and determined and very popular even without being pretty. Her thumbs did not bother her one bit. She had charm and audacity galore and usually got whatever she wanted. She decided early on to seek excitement and adventure. She wasn't about to let two strange little digits become an obstacle.

"In high school she got top grades, but found neither challenge nor excitement. It was more fun to hang around in unconventional circles, wear forbidden things like lipstick and eye makeup, and attend the theater, especially long after the curfew for proper young ladies. You know the rules for young ladies were very firm then. Rumors were that she smoked and even drank occasionally, and in very inappropriate places. And the company she kept was questionable too. Her parents were distraught but could not control her. Then her school threw her out for unladylike behavior."

"Oh? What did she do?"

"If I remember right, she was caught out on a school night after curfew hours, with makeup that was forbidden, in a nightclub on a date with a man, and it wasn't the first time. Her parents were very upset, but not Sofia.

She insisted the education she wanted was not to be found in school. If it scandalized the relatives, too bad!"

"And she got away with it?"

"Well, this young Zionist man she met in some club liked to kid around that her thumbs were outstanding instruments, perfectly designed by God himself for the pioneering life he intended for them. They were a sign of her ideal adaptability for work on the farms in the land that was destined to become Israel. Soon Sofia also became an ardent Zionist and what they called a free thinker. Together she and her young man attended clandestine meetings in secret locations. They schemed to emigrate from Poland to Palestine and to settle on some kibbutz there. Sofia even tried to persuade her family that they should all go."

"Why didn't they?"

"Are you kidding? They would not hear of it. Why would anyone want to leave the most active Jewish community in Eastern Europe for the wastelands and mosquito marshes of Palestine? But they changed their mind about Sofia when she became pregnant. She was sent away to Jerusalem in a real hurry then. Her boyfriend went too. For years the family hardly mentioned her except in hush-hush tones. The disgrace of pregnancy before marriage faded with the years. We knew she and her boyfriend married and had a healthy son. Sofia wrote that she and her husband worked hard in a kibbutz, but that she was happy there. She never came back to Poland. That's why she is alive!"

"What about your brother Leon? What made him leave Poland?"

"Well, Leon resented the fact that he was denied admission to a Polish school of engineering. He really had the grades, and he was bitterly disappointed. If it weren't for the fact that he was Jewish, he would almost certainly have been admitted. So after he was married, he and his wife decided that they would raise a family of their own in a friendlier country. They applied for a visa to the United States, but they were denied. Then they decided that anything was better than Poland, and they went to Brazil. They wrote that they were doing well and that they were blessed with a daughter and a son. Eventually they established a leather goods shop like our father's and then expanded into carnival supplies. They tried to persuade some of the rest of the family to join them, but who would want to live in the wilds of South America?"

"I know, that's why they are alive!"

I don't have to ask Mom about her brother Adam. I already know his story. He and his wife, Meriam, survived thanks to the kindness of a Polish family that hid them. In the heat of summer or cold of winter, sick and well, they spent a lot of their time under a bed. But they survived. I know that Meriam is pregnant now, and that she and Adam are already betting on what kind of a thumb their baby will have.

Just then Adam joins us. As soon as he realizes what the conversation is all about he sticks out his big hands, ugly thumbs up, and laughs. No question about it, he is my mother's brother.

"You know," Mom says, "If ever I should spot someone with thumbs like ours, I will be curious and excited. I know that now they are called club thumbs, but for me they will always be Honigstein thumbs. Very lucky Honigstein thumbs! I am sure to wonder if this person is a lost member of our family.

30

L'Chaim
Rachel, January 1948

There is peace in Mom's voice as she sings this old Polish folk tune. "Oh how delightful, to sway among the waves, to hear their 'shumi shumi' sound, and watch them drift away." Yes, it is so fitting as we sit on the deck of the Sobieski, the boat that is taking us to America. It is a Polish ship. Mom laughs at the irony of it, and keeps on humming. We continue to watch the waves drift away, farther and farther eastward, back toward the continent that we are most happy to leave.

It wasn't always so. Long, long ago, when she was young, Mom tells me that she dreamed of a world where religion was one's personal choice; where you could be friends with anybody, even marry them. But the Second World War extinguished our family and her dreams. She stopped believing in fables about a peaceful existence, especially in Poland, where even the graves marking the centuries of our existence were destroyed. When we smuggled ourselves out of there, none of us had a moment of regret.

Well, I understand about Poland and Germany, but what about France, where we leave behind Lillian, and Manya, and Grandpa Sam? And what about Adam and Meriam? And even though I know that the only survivors in Europe from our immediate family are Mom, her brother Adam, and myself, what about my father? I know he was almost certainly killed in the Warsaw Ghetto Uprising. But there is always a doubt. What if he was just wounded, or lost his memory. What if he does reappear? Mom tells me that I'm dreaming. That is not realistic. It would happen only in fairytales. And I'm too old for that. My mother's uncle, Joseph Richland from New York, paid a lot of money for our third-class passage on this boat. He was either smart or lucky, because he left Europe before the war. Mom does not remember him well, but she knew his name, and UNRA found him. He has agreed to be responsible for us in America, and to keep us off welfare. Thank you, Uncle Joseph.

We have all heard those tall stories about the golden apples that grow on the trees in America. Even I know they are silly. Actually, it is about all I know, except that when we were in the DP camp in Germany, a lot of our food came from America. Chocolate too. Often, when I saw an American soldier, he was handsome and smiling. Sometimes he was giving out chocolates to some of the boys and girls who were closest to him. I never got any. I don't like to seem like I'm begging, and I always stay in the back of the crowd. I'm just more comfortable there.

I'm not sure where the idea of not being safe in a crowd came from. But somehow I'm aware that crowds are big targets and stupid. They just follow and hope. They cannot hide. Both Mom and Moses were alone during the war, free to disappear as they thought best. Moses actually spent two years all by himself in a dugout in the forests of Poland and Lithuania. He even learned how to enter his hole in the ground without leaving footprints in the snow. I don't think I could ever do that.

But I did learn to keep myself inconspicuous when I felt in danger. So the idea of having an escape route helped us all to be here. Of course I'm mighty glad that my Mom survived and came to get me after the war. Where would I be without her?

The first couple of days on this ship I just stayed close to our dormitory, which is way below the deck. It's rather dim and crowded with lots of bunk beds and everybody's stuff. Then I decided to explore a little, and

Rachel at railing of the ship Sobieski coming to America. 1948

so I discovered the first class section. Wow, what a difference. Actually I did pass a sign that was supposed to warn me not to enter. I guess I just wasn't paying attention, and besides signs are sort of like crowds. You have to use your judgment. That one wasn't very intimidating.

I am still stunned at the difference. First class looks like a different ship on a different ocean. Everything is brighter there, even the light. I guess that is because it is on the top deck. Now I sneak in there whenever I can. Tablecloths, flowers, candles, elegantly dressed women and men in formal wear. Lots of jewelry—gold necklaces and rings everywhere. People swimming in a pool of warm water in the middle of winter.

There is one most talented family that especially fascinates me. They often perform on the stage in the first class. The mother sings opera and other songs. The little girl, probably no more than seven years old, dances in a little pink costume. Her brother, always dressed in a black velour suit, plays piano. Even when he is just walking around in the afternoon, he is wearing a fancy suit but with short pants. I can tell from the reaction of the listeners that he plays very well. They call him little Mozart. I'd love to get friendly with him and learn more about him and how he got to be such a good musician. Of course that's impossible. He and I are worlds apart in class and in fortune. I wonder, did he have very expensive lessons? Did he just learn to play by ear?

I know that my own grandparents, the Honigsteins, lived modestly but they still took vacations in the country. I know Mom had piano lessons too, although World War I cut them short. So maybe someday I will have a piano. Of course, I would no more expect to live like these "first class" people than I would expect to grow golden finger-nails. When I think of what might be once we are in America, I am reminded of "The Tango of the Prisoner," that song I learned in the Displaced Persons' Camp.

Once there were tangos, foxtrots, and waltzes,
Sung during enchanting times.

I sing the song to myself, imagining enchanting times, music, and peace.

In a few hours we will be landing in America. Lots of the people are leaning over the rail of the ship, searching the horizon. Laughter fills the air. The buzz of excitement explodes into bubbles of joy and song. I wriggle myself in next to my mom at the rail. When she turns to smile at me, I glimpse the yellow amber resting on her neck. She reaches out and draws me close.

APPENDIX

PHOTOGRAPHS

Meriam and Adam with their daughter, Dvora,
in Israel, 1950

Leonia's brother Louis and his wife Eva in
Brazil, 1951

Rochelle and nuns at Szymanow, 1989

Rochelle and Leonia, 1992

HONIGSTEIN FAMILY

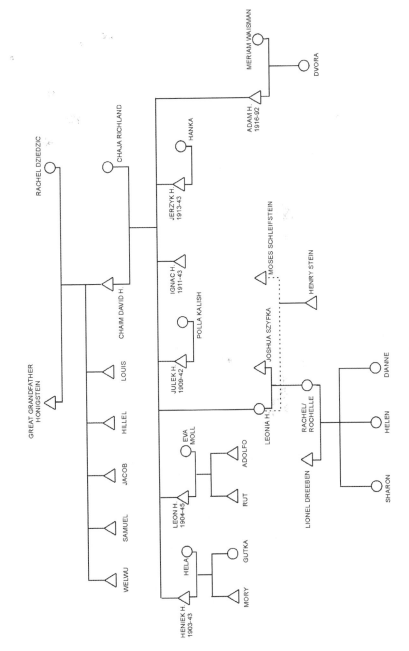

HISTORICAL BACKGROUND

1825–1856

Russia controls a large part of Poland. Emperor Nicholas I of Russia requires Jewish boys between twelve and eighteen years old to enlist in the army. Conscription period for those who are selected is up to twenty-five years. During that time 50,000 Jewish boys are taken by force from their homes. While they serve the Czar they are subjected to missionary activity to convert them to Christianity. Many succumb. Great-Grandpa Honigstein is one of the abducted youngsters. He is not heard of for twenty-five years. When he returns to his family, his own mother fails to recognize him. He marries Rachel Dziedzic, a much younger woman. They have ten children. Chaim David Honigstein is their youngest child.

1902

Chaim David Honigstein marries Chaya Richland. They have six sons—Hirsh/*Heniek**, Leibel/*Leon*, Julek, Itchak/*Ignac*, Jacob/*Jerzyk*, and Adam—and one daughter, Leonia.

1936

Leonia Honigstein marries Joshua/*Sevek* Szyfka. Daughter Rachel is born the following year. There is an escalation of harassment of Jews everywhere in Poland. It is encouraged by anti-Semitic propaganda. Gangs enter Jewish areas of Warsaw, harass and intimidate Jews, and overturn carriages with babies.

*Italicized names are the Polish equivalent of Hebrew names.

1939

September: Nazis bomb Warsaw for twenty days prior to occupying the country. At that time ten percent of the population of Poland, or about three million people, is Jewish. In Warsaw one-third of the population, or about 375,000, is Jewish.

1939

December 1: All Jews over twelve years old must wear a blue Star of David as an armband.

1940

Summer: Twenty-five percent of the Jewish population is conscripted to work for the Nazis.

October: The ghetto is established. All Jews are forced into one-tenth of the city's area. Jews brought in from outside of Warsaw exacerbate the crowding even more. Jews are forced to build the ghetto wall.

November: The ghetto is sealed. Jews cannot leave without special permits which are impossible to get. Any attempt to leave the ghetto is punishable by death.

1941

Ten percent of Jewish population dies as a result of malnutrition, disease, overcrowding, and expulsions.

1942

Deportation to death camps is in full swing. Between July 22 and September 12, 310,000 Jews are "resettled" to concentration camps. Most of them are executed.

1943: January–April

German soldiers entering the ghetto are surprised by resistance. They pull back to wait for reinforcements.

1944: April 19

Germans order final liquidation of the ghetto. Resistance continues for over a month until Germans order the torching of the entire ghetto.

1944: May 15

A German general writes, "The Jewish Quarter in Warsaw is no longer."

1945

German defeat.

1945–1947

Aftermath of the war. Ninety percent of Polish Jews have been murdered. Fewer than one half of one percent of the Jewish children of Warsaw survive.

31277624R00115

Made in the USA
San Bernardino, CA
06 March 2016